16 EXTRAORDINARY
AMERICAN
WOMEN

WITHDRAWN

EMMA HAHN

J. WESTON
WALCH
PUBLISHER

PORTLAND, MAINE

Photo Credits

Helen Keller	© 1937 AP/WIDE WORLD PHOTOS
Eleanor Roosevelt	© 1995 Courtesy of Franklin D. Roosevelt Library
Georgia O'Keeffe	© 1931 UPI/BETTMANN NEWSPHOTOS
Julia Morgan	© 1995 Special Collections, California Polytechnic State University
Wilma P. Mankiller	© 1988 UPI/BETTMANN
Rachel Carson	© 1963 AP/WIDE WORLD PHOTOS
Dorothea Lange	© 1995 the Dorothea Lange Collection, The Oakland Museum of California, the City of Oakland. Gift of Paul S. Taylor.
Rosalyn Sussman Yalow	© 1977 UPI/BETTMANN
Ella Fitzgerald	© 1995 WIDE WORLD PHOTOS
Ruth Bader Ginsberg	© 1995 AP/WIDE WORLD PHOTOS
Ka'iulani of Hawaii	© 1995 Courtesy of Hawaii State Archives
Barbara Jordan	© 1994 AP/WIDE WORLD PHOTOS
Donna Karan	© 1993 Malcolm Clarke /AP/WIDE WORLD PHOTOS
Elizabeth Cochrane Seaman (Nellie Bly)	© 1967 Dover Publications
Nikki Giovanni	© 1995 Elizabeth Isele
Bonnie Blair	© 1994 Dylan Martinez/REUTERS/BETTMANN

1   2   3   4   5   6   7   8   9   10

ISBN 0-8251-2808-0

Copyright © 1996
J. Weston Walch, Publisher
P.O. Box 658 • Portland, Maine 04104-0658

Printed in the United States of America

Contents

Preface

"Remember the Ladies"

"Remember the Ladies. Be more generous and favorable to them than your ancestors. Do not put such unlimited power in the hands of the Husbands. If particular care and attention is not paid to the Ladies, we are determined to foment a Rebellion, and will not hold ourselves bound by any Laws in which we have no voice, or Representation."

—*Abigail Adams*
1776

Introduction

Many women have made a great difference in American history. The ways in which they lived their lives have brought positive changes for all Americans. This book contains the stories of 16 women—from diverse economic, ethnic, racial, social, and geographic backgrounds. They are writers, artists, musicians, scientists, politicians, and businesswomen. Some of their voices you may know; others you may never have heard. Each has made an extraordinary contribution to America's rich heritage and to our lives today.

The 16 American women included in this book are:

- Helen Keller, Advocate for the blind
- Eleanor Roosevelt, Humanitarian
- Georgia O'Keeffe, Artist
- Julia Morgan, Architect
- Wilma P. Mankiller, Principal Chief, Cherokee Nation of Oklahoma
- Rachel Carson, Conservationist
- Dorothea Lange, Photojournalist
- Rosalyn Sussman Yalow, Nobel Prize-winning doctor

- Ella Fitzgerald, Singer
- Ruth Bader Ginsberg, Supreme Court Justice
- Ka'iulani of Hawaii, An "American" princess
- Barbara Jordan, Congresswoman
- Donna Karan, Fashion designer
- Elizabeth Cochrane Seaman (Nellie Bly), Journalist
- Nikki Giovanni, Poet
- Bonnie Blair, Speed skater

I hope you will enjoy reading these stories. As you read about these women's experiences, you may be able to imagine ways in which you, too, can make a difference. Each of our lives counts.

Helen Keller

Advocate for the Blind
(1880–1968)

Helen Keller

Helen Keller was born in Tuscumbia, Alabama, in 1880. Her father had been a captain in the Confederate Army and fought at the Siege of Vicksburg. Now he was a marshal and publisher of a weekly newspaper.

Helen's mother was a true southern belle from the city of Memphis. She was intelligent; she read a great deal and had an excellent memory.

When Helen was just 19 months old, she became very ill with an unknown disease. The disease left Helen blind, deaf, and dumb.

Before the illness, Helen had been a bright—even gifted—child. Afterwards, she became deeply frustrated by not being able to communicate with her family. Helen was wildly destructive. She often kicked and lashed out at anyone within reach.

Even so, Helen still showed her intelligence. She learned to make up hand signals for things she wanted. For example, if she wanted bread and butter, she mimicked the motions of cutting bread and spreading butter on it. She pretended to put on glasses to indicate her father; she sucked on her fingers to mean her baby sister. In all, Helen had over 60 of these signs.

When Helen was about six years old, her mother read about the Perkins Institute in Boston. The famous English author Charles Dickens had written about the institute. He described its successful work with a deaf and blind woman named Laura Bridgeman in his book *American Notes*.

Helen's mother thought that Laura's case was like Helen's. When she discussed the possibility with Helen's father, he suggested they first pay a visit to Dr. Alexander Graham Bell of Washington. Bell, inventor of the telephone, was interested in different ways to teach the deaf because his wife was deaf.

After meeting Helen, Dr. Bell suggested the Kellers write to the director of the Perkins Institute. They could ask if there was a teacher or governess who could come to Alabama to work with Helen.

There was. That teacher's name was Annie M. Sullivan—a recent graduate of the Perkins Institute herself. When Annie first met the wild and spoiled Helen, she knew her greatest problem would be "how to discipline and control her without breaking her spirit."

It was a difficult task. But Helen was bright. She quickly learned the alphabet letters and words that Annie spelled out in her hand. The problem was that Helen could not connect the words to anything real. The words were meaningless—until one day at the water pump. For the first time, Helen connected the feel of water from the pump with Annie's spelled-out word: W-A-T-E-R. It was a turning point.

Helen's mother learned Annie's sign language so she, too, could communicate with Helen. Soon Helen had learned over 400 words. She remembered all of them.

Annie also taught Helen how to write in a script called "square hand." Helen wrote with pencil and paper over a grooved writing pencil in her right hand and guiding the tip of it with a finger from her left hand.

Within a year Annie brought Helen to Boston to attend Perkins Institute. They stayed six years. Then they went to the Wright-Hamson School in New York. The school was famous for teaching spoken language to deaf children.

In 1896, at age 16, Helen enrolled in the Cambridge School for Young Ladies to prepare for Radcliffe College. She entered Radcliffe in 1890, taking a full schedule of courses. Annie went to every class with her. She spelled out the lectures in Helen's hand.

Helen graduated in four years, *cum laude*, with the extra notation "excellent in English letters." It was a huge achievement for a deaf and blind person.

Annie married John Macy, a Harvard University literature professor. The three lived together. Macy later helped Helen write her autobiography.

In addition to her writing, Helen worked hard to improve conditions for the blind. She and Annie toured the United States, talking about the benefits of educating deaf and blind people. In 1918 they went to Hollywood to make a film, *Deliverance*, based on Helen's life.

In 1924, the new American Foundation for the Blind asked Helen to help them raise funds. She did, and became the central spokesperson for the organization. She lobbied successfully in Washington, DC, for new laws for the blind.

In 1936 Annie Sullivan died. Helen had to face the world without her loyal "Teacher." It was difficult at first. But Helen continued to travel throughout the world to speak out for the blind.

Probably the most famous play about Annie's work with Helen is *The Miracle Worker*. This play was first produced in 1957. It later became a film.

Helen received many awards and honors in her lifetime. She was given an honorary degree from Harvard University—the first Harvard had ever awarded to a woman. One Helen was especially proud of, however, was the Presidential Medal of Freedom. It was presented to her by President Lyndon Baines Johnson.

On her eightieth birthday Helen was asked about her plans for the future. She said, "I will always—as long as I have breath—work for the handicapped."

And she did, until she died of heart disease in her home in 1968.

Remembering the Facts

1. Where was Helen Keller born?

2. What famous battle did her father fight in as a captain in the Confederate Army?

3. How old was Helen when she lost her sight and hearing?

4. Who was the famous English author who wrote about the Perkins Institute in Boston?

5. What was the name of the Perkins patient whose problems seemed so similar to Helen's?

6. Why was Alexander Graham Bell interested in teaching the deaf?

7. What was the name of Helen's teacher from the Perkins Institute?

8. What was the first word that had real meaning for Helen after she became deaf?

9. What was the special script Helen learned to write?

10. From what college did Helen graduate?

Understanding the Story

1. How did Helen learn to communicate after she became deaf and blind?

2. Who besides Annie Sullivan helped Helen overcome her handicaps?

Getting the Main Idea

Why do you think Helen Keller would make a good role model for young people today?

Applying What You've Learned

Close your eyes and plug your ears with cotton. Now try to write a paragraph describing someone or something only by your senses of touch and smell.

Eleanor Roosevelt

Humanitarian (1884–1962)

One of Eleanor's earliest memories was when she and her parents were on a cruise to Europe. Their ship collided with another ship in the fog and sank. Fortunately, all of the passengers were rescued by the other ship.

Eleanor was haunted by a fear of drowning for the rest of her life. But that was probably the only fear this remarkable woman could not overcome. One of her favorite mottoes was, "You must do the thing you think you cannot do."

Eleanor was born on October 11, 1884. Her mother and father were very wealthy New Yorkers.

Eleanor Roosevelt

Her father was a handsome sportsman, and her mother was very beautiful—but not a warm and loving person. "My mother was troubled by my lack of beauty," Eleanor wrote in her autobiography. "She tried to instill perfect manners in me to make up for my ugly-duckling appearance."

Eleanor had two younger brothers, one of whom died of diphtheria before he was two.

Just before Eleanor's eighth birthday, her mother went into the hospital for surgery. While there, she caught diphtheria. She died at age 29. Eleanor's mother had asked that Eleanor's grandmother raise her children in the event of her death.

Eleanor and her father wrote beautiful letters to each other until he, too, died when she was ten.

Grandmother's house was a rather gloomy place. She had raised four children of her own and was exhausted by the time Eleanor came along. She always found it easiest to say no to anything Eleanor or her brother might ask.

Eleanor's life changed completely when she was 15. She went to Allenswood, a private school near London, England. The head-mistress, Marie Souvestre, was a gifted teacher. Eleanor said, "She shocked me into thinking, and that was a very good thing."

Eleanor spent three of the happiest years of her life at Allenswood. She would have stayed another year, but at 18 she had to come back to New York to prepare for her debut. It was usual for wealthy young girls to "come out," or be presented to society at a gala ball in New York City.

Eleanor was soon bored with just a social life. She began to do volunteer work in schools. She also joined a reform group called the Consumers League. They investigated working conditions among young women in New York. Eleanor visited factories where girls worked 12 to 14 hours a day, 6 days a week, for $6 a week. She also visited "sweatshops," where little children four and five years old worked at tables until they dropped in exhaustion.

In 1902, Eleanor met her cousin Franklin D. Roosevelt on a train. They fell in love and were married in 1905. Eleanor's Uncle Ted (Theodore Roosevelt) was now president; he gave the bride away.

Franklin entered politics in 1910 by running for the New York State Senate and winning. Eleanor and Franklin now had three children. The whole family moved to the state capital, Albany. Their house became a popular meeting place for politicians. Franklin valued Eleanor's opinions on many different issues.

Shortly into his second term as senator, Franklin was appointed Assistant Secretary of the Navy. This time the family moved to Washington, DC. Eleanor gave birth to two more children there. She took an active part in how her children were raised. She remembered how lonely her childhood had been; she did not want her children to feel the same.

In 1920 Franklin left the Navy Department to run for vice president of the United States. This was the first election in which women had the right to vote. So Franklin asked Eleanor to join him on the campaign trail. Roosevelt lost, but that was just the beginning of national politics for both Franklin and Eleanor.

In the summer of 1921, Franklin came down with polio. He recovered, but his legs were paralyzed forever. While he was recovering, Eleanor traveled about. She made visits and lectures to keep the Roosevelt name in the public eye.

Then, in 1928, Franklin was elected governor of New York. Since Franklin could not walk, Eleanor became his eyes and ears. She went to places he could not inspect. She became an expert on judging people's well-being—at school, work, or any other place.

In 1932 Franklin was elected President of the United States. Eleanor surprised people by being more than just a president's wife and White House hostess. She often met with the press. She invited women reporters only, since they were often edged out of the president's press conferences.

Eleanor was the first president's wife to fly. Again acting as Franklin's eyes and ears, she visited coal miners in Appalachia, migrant workers in California, slum dwellers in Puerto Rico, and poor sharecroppers in the South. She cared about people's problems.

She also cared about racial injustice. Eleanor said of America, "We have poverty that enslaves and racial prejudice that does the same."

Franklin was the first president ever elected for four terms. Eleanor was at his side for every one. During World War II she traveled around the world to comfort our troops and work for peace. She did not slow down after Franklin died in 1945.

The new president, Harry S. Truman, asked Eleanor to join the U.S. delegation to the first General Assembly of the United Nations. She was a member for eight years. She helped to create the Universal Declaration of Human Rights. The document still stands today, outlining the rights which people around the globe should have.

Eleanor continued to advise leaders—kings, queens, and presidents. John F. Kennedy would not even run for president without her approval. She died in 1962. Eleanor Roosevelt is remembered as a great humanitarian—truly a "First Lady of the World."

Remembering the Facts

1. What was Eleanor's greatest fear in life?

2. Did Eleanor have any brothers and sisters?

3. What caused Eleanor's mother's death?

4. What was Eleanor's favorite school?

5. What was Franklin D. Roosevelt's first elected office?

6. When Franklin was appointed Assistant Secretary of the Navy, where did he and Eleanor move?

7. What was the name of the disease that left Franklin's legs paralyzed?

8. What year was Franklin first elected President of the United States?

9. What did President Truman want Eleanor to do?

10. Which U.S. president asked for Eleanor's approval before he ran for office?

Understanding the Story

1. Do you think Eleanor had a happy childhood?

2. Why do you think so many people asked Eleanor for her advice?

Getting the Main Idea

Why do you think Eleanor Roosevelt would make a good role model for young people today?

Applying What You've Learned

Write a short paragraph to say what you would do if you were married to the president of the United States. (Boys can do this too, because someday there will probably be a woman president of the United States.)

Georgia O'Keeffe

Artist (1887–1986)

Georgia O'Keeffe, who would have been 100 if she had lived another year, was one of America's greatest artists.

Her paintings—boldy beautiful shapes of flowers, bones, mountains, and clouds—show the classic order hidden in nature.

O'Keeffe was born on a farm in Sun Prairie, Wisconsin. She was one of seven children. Georgia was first attracted to painting when she saw a framed watercolor of a red rose that her grandmother had painted.

Georgia O'Keeffe

In 1902, when Georgia was 15, her family moved to Williamsburg, Virginia. The principal of the private school she attended there was one of the first to recognize the young artist's talent. Instead of forcing Georgia to do class art work, she encouraged her to paint whatever she wanted. Later she told Georgia's mother that she thought Georgia should go on to art school.

Her mother agreed, and Georgia began studying at the Art Students League in New York City. There she learned to appreciate paint and color from the famous artist William Merritt Chase.

Georgia studied further with Alon Bement at the University of Virginia. There she learned about Oriental design and the balance between light and dark. She also learned the importance of filling the canvas with careful attention to the space between shapes. And she studied the post-Impressionist artists, especially Wassily Kandinsky. From this study, Georgia learned how colors and shapes can have lives of their own—not tied to real objects.

At Columbia Teachers College in New York City, Georgia first learned how to draw while listening to music. She began with simple charcoal sketches, then moved on to watercolors. To support herself while learning to paint, she taught art.

In 1915, when she had created a small body of work, Georgia shut herself in a room and placed all her paintings against the walls. If any looked too much like another painter's work, she threw them out. She wanted to express her ideas and hers alone.

She sent the sketches she had kept to an old school friend, Anita Pollitzer. Georgia thought only Pollitzer would see the sketches. So, she was horrified to learn that Pollitzer had shown them to the famous photographer Alfred Steiglitz. He was so excited about Georgia's work that he hung the sketches in his art gallery. Georgia was furious and demanded he take them down. Steiglitz convinced her not only that they should stay up, but also that she should marry him. Six months later she did.

They lived in New York City and on a farm in Lake George, New York. Georgia O'Keeffe painted in both places. This is when she first started painting giant close-up images of flowers. Some filled the whole canvas.

Steiglitz took over 500 photographs of O'Keeffe. It was a good marriage, but O'Keeffe was beginning to feel her creativity stifled in the city. It was too crowded and too noisy for her. She also became bored with Lake George, saying, "The people live such pretty little lives, and the scenery is such little, pretty scenery."

In 1929, she was invited to spend her first summer in Taos, New Mexico. After that she returned every summer until 1940. Then she bought her own ranch in Abiquiu, New Mexico. After Steiglitz died in 1946, O'Keeffe never came back to New York for very long. She loved the wild country in New Mexico and continued to paint her beloved mountains until she died.

O'Keeffe once said that courage—or nerve—is the first thing an artist needs to get on in life. O'Keeffe never gave up her nerve. She often broke the rules. She became a fine artist when women were expected only to teach art. And, instead of painting delicate bouquets or garden flowers, she filled huge canvases with thick, colored paints. She was in her seventies when she took her first raft trip down the Colorado River!

Georgia O'Keeffe's paintings inspire all artists to look for what is unique or different in ordinary everyday things.

Remembering the Facts

1. What kinds of things did Georgia like to paint?

2. What was the name of the town in Wisconsin where O'Keeffe was born?

3. What was the subject of her grandmother's painting?

4. Who first suggested Georgia should go on to art school?

5. What was the name of the famous painter with whom Georgia studied at the Art Students League in New York?

6. What did Georgia learn from her study of Kandinsky?

7. Where did Georgia learn to draw while listening to music?

8. What did Georgia sketch with before she took up watercolor paints?

9. What kind of work did Georgia O'Keeffe's husband do?

10. What was the name of the place where O'Keeffe bought a farm in New Mexico?

Understanding the Story

1. Many of the people who supported Georgia O'Keeffe's career in art were women. How did these women help change her life?

2. How do you think O'Keeffe's growing up on a farm in Wisconsin influenced her artwork?

Getting the Main Idea

Why do you think Georgia O'Keeffe would be a good role model for young people today?

Applying What You've Learned

Georgia O'Keeffe was a very strong and independent woman. Do you think these are two important qualities for a leader to have? Write a paragraph explaining your answer.

Julia Morgan

Architect (1872–1957)

Julia Morgan's trailblazing career opened the world of architecture to women.

She was born in San Francisco in 1872 and raised across the bay in Oakland, California. Julia's father worked, but the family's wealth came from money her mother had inherited.

Julia had one sister and three brothers. Her mother thought her daughters and sons should have equal opportunities. Both Julia and her sister excelled in school. But Julia wanted to excel physically, too. Julia was small and often sick. So she stole time for secret workouts on her brothers' gym equipment to build up her strength.

Julia Morgan

After graduating from Oakland High School, Julia enrolled at the University of California at Berkeley. Going to college was unusual for a woman at this time. Julia stretched tradition a little further by becoming the first woman to study architecture in the university's College of Engineering. She had always loved talking with her mother's cousin, Pierre LeBrun, the architect who designed the Metropolitan Life Insurance Tower in New York City. Fascinated by his work, she wanted to learn more about it.

In her last year at the university, she met Bernard Maybeck. He became one of the most important people in her life. Maybeck was teaching geometry at the university and giving architecture lessons in his home. He had studied at the École des Beaux Arts in Paris; Julia was determined to go there too.

After graduation, she worked for Maybeck for two years. Then she left for Paris, where she studied for two more years. She passed the entrance exams to get into the École des Beaux Arts. Finally, in 1898, she was the first woman admitted to their school of architecture. However, they made Julia sit out of sight, behind a screen, in all her classes. Four years later, Julia was the first woman to graduate from the École des Beaux Arts.

She returned to California, where she was the first woman to receive an architect's license. Two of Julia's first jobs were designing buildings for the University of California at Berkeley campus. It was lucky that another woman was financing these projects for the university. Her name was Phoebe Apperson Hearst, mother of the famous newspaper publisher William Randolph Hearst.

Phoebe Hearst asked Julia to redesign her own home. She also gave her several other commissions. It may have been Hearst who convinced Julia to open her own office in San Francisco.

Julia certainly received a lot of business from recommendations made by Phoebe Hearst. She also received work from other women and women's organizations. They were especially proud to be able to offer their assignments to a woman. She designed many buildings from San Diego to San Francisco, and from Salt Lake City to Honolulu, for the YWCA.

The job that truly established Julia Morgan's career was to rebuild the elegant Fairmont Hotel. It had been ruined in the 1906 earthquake. Keeping the basic idea of the old structure, Julia rebuilt the hotel in a grand fashion. Today it is still considered one of the most beautiful buildings in San Francisco.

Now, Morgan was in great demand to design houses, public buildings, hotels, churches, and schools. Besides her work for the University of California, she also designed many buildings at Mills, a college for women in Oakland. Her favorite style was Spanish revival, but she also worked often with natural red shingles. St. John's Presbyterian Church in Berkeley was a huge shingled structure that she built between 1908 and 1910. It is an architectural landmark in Berkeley.

Morgan had to take on assistants to help with all the work. She tried to hire women whenever possible. She also gave money anonymously to help women students wishing to study architecture.

After World War I, Morgan took on more work from Phoebe's son, William Randolph Hearst. In all, he commissioned nearly one third of the work of her entire career. She designed the family compound at San Simeon, on the coast of California between Los Angeles and San Francisco. The job was especially challenging, because Julia's design had to use parts of castles and monasteries that Hearst had brought back from Europe for his estate! The project took 20 years to complete. Today San Simeon is a California historic monument.

Hearst gave Julia Morgan so much work that she had to increase the number of her assistants to 35. She even hired an airplane and pilot.

Her work slowed down during World War II, when it was difficult to get building materials. Julia retired in 1946. She traveled throughout the world until her death in 1957.

Julia Morgan established the red shingle style in the San Francisco Bay area. She is recognized as one of the great architects in U.S. history. She was the first woman admitted to the American Institute of Architects in 1921. Throughout her career, she designed over 800 structures that still influence design and form today. She never married; architecture was her life.

Remembering the Facts

1. Where was Julia born?

2. How did she try to build up her physical heath?

3. What was the name of her mother's cousin who designed the Metropolitan Life Insurance Tower in New York City?

4. What was the name of the school in Paris that Julia attended after her graduation from the University of California?

5. What kind of publisher was William Randolph Hearst?

6. What was Julia's first important commission?

7. Julia designed St. John's Presbyterian Church in Berkeley to be built out of what natural materials?

8. How many years did it take to build San Simeon?

9. How much of Julia's work did William Randolph Hearst commission over her lifetime?

10. How many structures did Julia design before she retired?

Understanding the Story

1. Why was Julia so supportive of other women who wanted to study?

2. What is most memorable about Julia's architectural designs?

Getting the Main Idea

Why do you think Julia Morgan would be a good role model for young people today?

Applying What You've Learned

Write a short paragraph about how you would feel if your teacher moved your desk behind a screen in the classroom. What would you do to keep it from getting you down?

Wilma P. Mankiller

Principal Chief, Cherokee Nation of Oklahoma (1945–   )

Wilma P. Mankiller is the first woman ever to serve as chief of a major North American Indian tribe. All 92,000 Cherokees vote to elect their chief. The only larger North American tribe is the Navajo.

Wilma was born in 1945 on the Cherokee reservation land in Tahlequah, Oklahoma. Her mother, Irene, is white, her father, Charlie, is full-blooded Cherokee.

The name *Mankiller* was an honorary title given to one of Wilma's Cherokee ancestors for his success in battles.

Wilma grew up on the 160 acres the United States government gave to her grandfather. He got the land after the government

Wilma P. Mankiller

forced the Cherokee people to move from their homes in the southeastern United States in 1838. The government marched the Cherokee west to "Indian Territory" in Oklahoma. Their path is known as the "Trail of Tears," because several thousand Cherokee died along the route. It was a sad time in American history.

Wilma's early life was not much easier than that of her ancestors. Her family suffered many hardships after they were forced to move. The new land was not fertile, and Wilma's family was very poor. A small house provided a roof over their heads—but not much room for two parents and 11 children. Plus, there was no indoor plumbing or electricity.

The family suffered from another forced relocation when Wilma was 12 years old. A severe drought finally made it impossible for the Mankillers to farm their 160 acres of reservation land. So the U.S. government forced them to move to San Francisco. There was a new federal program for putting rural Indians into American cities. Wilma said, "They told us it would be a better life."

"But it was hard!" Wilma said. "How can you be on the reservation one day, and try to deal with a city, television, indoor plumbing, neon lights, and elevators the next?"

Her father worked in the warehouses of San Francisco. He became a union activist.

Wilma married a wealthy man from Ecuador. They had two children.

In 1969 Wilma became active in the American Native Rights Movement. Indian demonstrators took over the former Alcatraz Prison, built out in the middle of San Francisco Bay. They were protesting the horrible treatment of American Indians by the U.S. government. The Native American protesters occupied the prison for 18 months. Wilma helped to raise money for them.

After this, Wilma started going to college at night. She became the Native American programs' coordinator for the Oakland public schools.

In the 1970's, Wilma divorced her husband. She moved her two children back to her grandfather's homestead on the reservation in Oklahoma. She built a small wooden house to shelter her family on the property.

Wilma got a job working for the Cherokee Nation. She finished her college degree at Flaming Arrow University in Stillwater, Oklahoma. Then she became director of community development for the Cherokee Nation. She raised money for the tribe to build better water systems and better housing.

She was so successful that Ross Swimmer, then the Principal Chief of the Cherokee, asked her to be his running mate as Assistant Chief in the 1983 elections. They won. Then Ross Swimmer was appointed head of the Bureau of Indian Affairs in Washington, DC, in 1985. Wilma became the Cherokee Nation's first female chief.

Wilma married again. Her husband, Charlie Soap, was a Cherokee who also worked in rural development. When Wilma had to run for election in 1987, Charlie campaigned hard for her. It was a close vote, because many members of the tribe were not sure how they felt about having a woman chief. But Wilma won.

She worked to lower her people's jobless rate. She lobbied successfully for better health services and education for the tribe.

Wilma established the Cherokee Nation's Chamber of Commerce and a Cherokee Literacy Institute. She wanted members of the tribe to be able to read and write in their own language so they would not lose their heritage. "Most people," she said, "deal with us as though we were in a museum or a history book."

Wilma knows that one of the greatest problems for her people is the loss of their self-esteem. Ever since the "Trail of Tears" march, the Cherokee have felt helpless in the face of U.S. government demands.

Wilma has received many awards and honors, including "Woman of the Year" from *Ms.* magazine in 1987. Today Wilma and her family still live in the small house she built on her grandfather's homestead. When she was asked what she would like to be remembered for, Wilma said, "I want to be remembered as the person who helped us [the Cherokee] restore faith in ourselves."

Wilma has accomplished this—and more—in her life. Unfortunately, she was nearly killed in an automobile accident in 1979. She had 17 operations after the accident in order to correct all of the injuries. At that time, doctors discovered that Wilma had muscular dystrophy. Still, this extraordinary American woman works as hard as ever to improve her people's way of life.

Remembering the Facts

1. What is the only North American Indian tribe that is larger than the Cherokee?

2. What state was Wilma born in?

3. How many acres did the U.S. government give her grandfather?

4. What is the name of the path over which the U.S. government force-marched the Cherokee?

5. What was the name of the second city where the Mankillers were forced to relocate?

6. What country was Wilma's first husband from?

7. What is the name of the old prison in San Francisco Bay where Native Americans demonstrated in 1969?

8. What was the name of the Principal Chief who first asked Wilma to run as his Assistant Chief?

9. What is the name of the magazine that named Wilma "Woman of the Year" in 1987?

10. What disease did doctors discover Wilma had?

Understanding the Story

1. Why do the Cherokee suffer from low self-esteem?

2. What huge problems have challenged Wilma as she tries to improve life for her people?

Getting the Main Idea

Why do you think Wilma Mankiller would be a good role model for young people today?

Applying What You've Learned

If someone from another country forced you out of your house and tried to erase your language, your holidays, and your traditions, what would you do to keep your spirits up and your cultural heritage alive?

Rachel Carson

Conservationist (1907–1964)

In 1963 Rachel Carson was a quiet, dedicated author and conservationist. She was famous for her books about marine biology—life under the sea and along the sea-shore. But her new book, *Silent Spring*, warned us about the horrifying things that chemical pesticides did to the natural environment. The book caused an uproar.

In *Silent Spring*, Carson proved beyond all doubt that powerful pesticides were as dangerous to life on earth as nuclear war. People—especially

Rachel Carson

those connected with the giant $250 million pesticide industry—were outraged. CBS television scheduled a special show to inter-view Rachel Carson. But three of the five sponsors withdrew their support before the show went on the air.

Farmers had always used some form of pesticides before World War II. However, they did little damage to the environment. After the war, new pesticides many times more toxic than the earlier ones were used. In 1960 alone, over 638 million pounds of these deadly chemicals were dumped into the environment.

Rachel Carson was born in Springdale, Pennsylvania, in 1907. It was hundreds of miles from the ocean, but Rachel always felt her "destiny was somehow linked with the sea."

Having been a teacher, Rachel's mother loved teaching Rachel how to become more aware of the beauty and mystery in the natural world. Rachel said, "I can remember no time when I wasn't interested in the out-of-doors and the whole of the world of nature . . . I was a solitary child and spent a great deal of time in woods and beside streams, learning the birds and the insects and the flowers."

Rachel also loved books. She thought she would be a writer. In fact, she had her first story published in the famous magazine *St. Nicholas* when she was ten.

She went to public schools until she went to Pennsylvania College for Women (later Chatham College). Rachel studied English, thinking that was the best way to become a writer.

She reached a major turning point in her life when she had to take a course in biology to graduate from college. She was fascinated, and decided to major in biology instead of English. Rachel had always wanted to write, but she was worried she did not have enough imagination to do it successfully. "Biology," she said, "has given me something to write about. I will try in my writing to make animals in the woods and waters where they live as alive and as meaningful to others as they are to me."

Women were not encouraged to study science in the 1920's. But Rachel did. She graduated *magna cum laude* in 1929. Then, with the help of one of her science teachers (another woman), Rachel got a scholarship from Johns Hopkins University for graduate study in zoology.

The best part of her studies, however, were the summers she spent at the Marine Biological Laboratory, a center for marine research in Woods Hole, Massachusetts. Rachel loved the ocean; its creatures and plants fascinated her. More than ever, she knew she wanted to be a marine zoologist.

In 1935 both her father and her married older sister died suddenly. Rachel had to support her aging mother and her sister's two orphaned sons. She found a job writing scripts for a radio program about marine life for the U.S. Bureau of Fisheries.

People were so pleased with Rachel Carson's scripts that they asked her to write more. She published "Undersea," an article about ocean life, in the famous literary magazine the *Atlantic Monthly* in 1937.

Carson published her first book, *Under the Sea-Wind*, in 1941. It talks about ecology by showing the many different ways in which animals depend on one another. Critics praised the book; it was Carson's favorite of all her work.

Because so much of World War II was fought on—and under— the sea, a new interest in oceanic research began. Knowledge of tides, currents, and topography of the ocean bottom were important to waging war at sea.

The Bureau of Fisheries became the U.S. Fish and Wildlife Service. Rachel Carson was an important person there. As Assistant to the Chief of the Office of Information, all new research in oceanography had to cross her desk.

She was one of the first two women allowed to join the crew of *Albatross III*, the U.S. government's marine research vessel.

In 1950 Carson published her second book, *The Sea Around Us*. This one is about the world's oceans, from their origins billions of years ago to the present day. The book was a huge success. It won many awards (including the National Book Award), was a best-seller in the United States, and was translated into 32 different languages for publication around the world.

The Edge of the Sea was her book about the ecology of shore life along the Atlantic seaboard. It was published in 1955 and also became a best-seller.

Silent Spring was very different from her earlier books. Carson knew that her arguments against using such deadly pesticides as

DDT would create great controversy. But she could not remain silent.

President John F. Kennedy read her book. He ordered his Science Advisory Committee to create a special panel to investigate the effects of pesticides on the environment.

Rachel Carson died of cancer two years after the book's publication. She was not aware of the many awards and honors it received. One that would have made her especially proud came from Supreme Court Justice William O. Douglas. He said, "*Silent Spring* is the most important chronicle of this century for the human race."

Certainly, the environmental movement as we know it today owes much to the courage of this extraordinary American woman.

Remembering the Facts

1. What was the name of Rachel Carson's most controversial book?

2. What did she argue was destroying the environment?

3. What TV network had scheduled a special program on Rachel Carson and her book?

4. Where was Rachel born?

5. What was the name of the magazine where Rachel published her first story?

6. What was the college course that turned Rachel into a science writer?

7. Where was the Marine Biological Laboratory at which Rachel studied for many summers?

8. Rachel got a scholarship from which university for graduate study in zoology?

9. What was the name of the U.S. government's marine research vessel that Carson was allowed to join as a crew member?

10. What was the name of Carson's first book?

Understanding the Story

1. Why did Rachel find marine zoology so rewarding?

2. Do you think Rachel was against people who make their living from pesticides? Or was she against what the pesticides do to the environment?

Getting the Main Idea

Why do you think Rachel Carson would make a good role model for young people today?

Applying What You've Learned

It can be very hard to take a stand against something that makes money for people. If you knew that something that made people wealthy was also damaging our world, how would you argue on behalf of the world?

Dorothea Lange

Photographer (1895–1965)

Dorothea Lange

When Dorothea Lange was 17, she knew she wanted to become a photographer. She had never owned a camera, or even taken a picture. But she knew this was what she wanted to do with her life.

Dorothea was born in Hoboken, New Jersey, in 1895. Her mother worked as a librarian in New York City, just across the river from Hoboken. Dorothea went to a school that was close to her mother's library on the Lower East Side. Every day after school, Dorothea would wait in the library until she and her mother could go home together.

The Lower East Side neighborhood was crammed full of immigrants from all over the world. Dorothea could look into their tenement houses from the library windows. She saw people talking, cooking, washing and sewing, working and eating. "I looked into lives so strange to me."

Dorothea watched and learned. She used her eyes like a camera, focusing on details: people's faces, hands, the way they stood, the way they related to one another. She studied the major parts of a picture to understand people's lives.

Dorothea was shy and quiet. She felt out of place among the immigrant children in her school. An early bout with polio had damaged her leg. She always walked with a limp; this also made her feel like an outsider.

When Dorothea was 12, her father left home. He never visited or wrote Dorothea. He never sent money to help support her and her mother. Dorothea's mother was so busy working that she did not have time to keep track of Dorothea. Dorothea enjoyed this freedom. She liked school, but she also liked being able to roam the streets of New York looking at all the different people. She visited Central Park and the Museum of Natural History. She went to plays and art shows.

Dorothea's grandmother, Sophie, taught her to look at objects. She told Dorothea, "Of all the beautiful things in the world, nothing is finer than an orange. Look at how perfect it is just as a thing in itself."

When Dorothea graduated from high school, she announced that she wanted to make pictures. Her mother was worried. She had never heard of a woman photographer. Young women in the early 1900's might get a teaching job, but a photography job was out of the question.

But, Dorothea persuaded the famous portrait photographer Arnold Genthe to hire her as an apprentice. Dorothea got her first assignment when a call came into the studio one day when no one else was able to go take the photograph. She did it with a big 8- by 10-inch camera. Both the customer and the studio were pleased with her work.

At this time Dorothea was taking a class at Columbia University. It was taught by another famous photographer, Clarence H. White. White taught Dorothea Lange the fine points of photographing people.

A year later, Dorothea and a friend left New York City for San Francisco. She began doing some portrait work for a store there. Her pictures were such a success that she soon opened her own studio. She had a reputation for being honest and truthful. Her portraits show more than just subjects; they show people's lives.

In 1920 she married an artist named Maynard Dixon. They had two sons, Daniel and John. But neither Dorothea nor Maynard let the children interfere with their artwork. Maynard was away for long periods of time. Dorothea sometimes let others take care of her boys if she wanted to work.

Then, in the fall of 1929, the stock market crashed. The Great Depression began. Within a year, one out of every four people was jobless. People could no longer afford luxuries such as Dorothea's portraits or Maynard's paintings.

One day while looking out her studio window, Dorothea saw a drifter walk by. Curious to find out where he was going, she followed him down the street. He was in line with a number of other people waiting for free food. Dorothea went back for her camera. She took one of her most famous photographs, "White Angel Bread Line."

Suddenly Dorothea knew that real life was in the streets—not in her studio. She began with photographs of jobless people in San Francisco, including longshoremen on the waterfront and homeless people. Her new photographs were called "documentary" photos— from the Latin word *docere*, meaning "to teach."

Paul Taylor, a professor, saw Dorothea's work. He was interested in improving living conditions for the migrant workers in California. Taylor had written often about their horrible living conditions, with no result. But when Dorothea photographed the conditions, her photos got the point across. Another of her most famous photographs, "Migrant Mother," was taken at this time. Her picture of the hungry, desperate-looking migrant mother and her children moved the government to action to improve the lot of migrant workers.

Dorothea Lange's work was praised by Eleanor Roosevelt. She received more assignments from Washington. She and Paul Taylor were sent by the Farm Security Administration to photograph and report on farmers and migrant workers all over California, Oklahoma, and the rural South.

Dorothea Lange received one of the first Guggenheim Fellowships awarded to a photographer to "photograph the American Social Scene." She spent her entire life photographing people. When she died, Dorothea left us an extraordinary collection of photographs. She also left a vision of photography as a lens through which we can explore, reveal, and understand the human condition. That way we can try to improve the quality of people's lives.

Remembering the Facts

1. How old was Dorothea when she knew she wanted to be a photographer?

2. What kind of work did her mother do?

3. What caused Dorothea's limp?

4. What was the name of Dorothea's grandmother?

5. What object did Dorothea's grandmother believe was one of the most beautiful in the world?

6. Who was the famous portrait photographer who took Dorothea on as an apprentice?

7. At what university in New York City did Dorothea study photography?

8. Where did Dorothea open her first studio?

9. What was the "White Angel Bread Line"?

10. Who was the artist Dorothea married?

Understanding the Story

1. Why did Dorothea feel like an outsider when she was growing up in New York City?

2. Why do you think Dorothea photographed people instead of places?

Getting the Main Idea

Why do you think Dorothea Lange would be a good role model for young people today?

Applying What You've Learned

Write a brief paragraph describing a person. Then draw a picture of that same person. Which example do you believe best gets your point across?

Rosalyn Sussman Yalow

Nobel Prize-Winning Doctor
(1921–   )

Rosalyn Sussman Yalow

The Nobel Prize is one of the world's greatest awards. It is named after Alfred Nobel of Sweden, who became a millionaire after he invented dynamite. Perhaps Nobel felt guilty about having invented such a deadly weapon. Before he died, he said, "I want all my money to be used to establish an annual award for the person who has done the most to benefit the world community."

The first awards were given in 1901. Since then, nearly 500 have been awarded to scientists—but only ten have been women. Rosalyn Yalow was one of those women. In 1977, she became the second woman ever to win the prize in medicine.

Dr. Yalow was honored for her development of RIA, or radioimmunoassay. This is a test used to measure hormones, viruses, enzymes, drugs, and hundreds of other biological substances to help detect disease.

Dr. Yalow and her colleague, Dr. Solomon A. Berson, discovered RIA by chance. They had been trying to measure the amount of insulin in adult diabetics. The doctors quickly realized that RIA could detect and measure insulin. By using radioscope tracers, the RIA could measure more accurately (to a billionth of a gram) than any other process.

One of the members of the Nobel committee said the accuracy of RIA was like being able to detect "half a lump of sugar in a lake about 62 miles long and wide and 10 miles deep"! Today, RIA is used to test for hundreds of different medical problems in thousands of laboratories around the world.

Rosalyn Sussman was born in the Bronx, New York, on July 19, 1921. Her parents, Clara and Simon, were first-generation Americans. Clara's large family had moved to the Bronx from Germany. Simon's family had come from the Ukraine to the Lower East Side of New York City.

Simon started his own paper and twine business. He married Clara and they had two children, Alex and Rosalyn. They were poor, but they made the most of what they had. There was some money for Saturday movies and baseball games. For other entertainment, Rosalyn and Alex would go to the free public library once a week and load up on books.

Rosalyn was a bright child. She taught herself to read before kindergarten. She loved math and was very good at it, skipping several grades along the way.

When she was eight she started helping her mother with her home sewing business after school. They made collars for women's dresses; Rosalyn's job was to turn the pieces of cloth while her mother ironed them.

Rosalyn went to an all-girls' junior and senior high school. She loved all math and science, but especially logic. She liked to sort out problems and puzzles.

At 15, she graduated and entered Hunter College in New York City. After taking her first physics course and reading about Madame Curie, she knew she wanted to devote her life to physics.

Rosalyn graduated with highest honors as Hunter College's first physics major. She wanted to continue her studies in graduate school. But all of her applications were turned down because she was a woman and a Jew. The schools said she'd never be able to get a job with two such handicaps.

Finally, Rosalyn accepted a secretarial job at Columbia University. She knew this job would allow her to take graduate courses at Columbia—for free. Then, finally, she was offered a position as a teaching assistant at the University of Illinois.

She was the only woman in the College of Engineering at Illinois, and only one of three Jews. Another was Aaron Yalow. They met on the first day of graduate school and were married two years later.

After receiving their Ph.D.'s in physics from Illinois in 1945, the Yalows moved back to the Bronx. Rosalyn returned to Hunter College as a physics professor until 1950. Then she was appointed physicist and assistant chief of the hospital's radioscope service. This is where she first began her joint research work with Dr. Solomon A. Berson. Their research partnership lasted 22 years, until his death in 1972. Had he lived, Dr. Berson could have shared the prize with Dr. Yalow. (The prize is never awarded to someone who has died.)

In 1976 Dr. Yalow was the first woman ever to win the Albert Lasker Prize for Basic Medical Research—just one year before she received the Nobel Prize.

Speaking for all women at the Nobel ceremony, Dr. Yalow said, "We must believe in ourselves or no one will. We must match our aspirations with competence, determination, and courage to succeed, and we must feel a personal responsibility to ease the path of those who come after us."

Remembering the Facts

1. To whom is the Nobel Prize given?

2. What was the name of the man who created the Nobel Prize?

3. What was his invention?

4. Where was Dr. Yalow born?

5. Where were her mother and father born?

6. What kind of business did Rosalyn's mother have at home?

7. What did Rosalyn do to help her mother's business?

8. Rosalyn graduated from what college as its first physics professor?

9. What kind of job did Rosalyn have to take at Columbia University in order to study there?

10. What do the initials RIA stand for?

Understanding the Story

1. Dr. Yalow had to deal with a great deal of prejudice during the course of her career. How do you think she was able to overcome this and go on to help others?

2. RIA was discovered by accident while Dr. Yalow and Dr. Berson were investigating another medical problem. How do you think scientists keep their minds open for such new discoveries while they are working on other problems?

Getting the Main Idea

Why do you think Dr. Rosalyn Yalow would be a good role model for the youth of today?

Applying What You've Learned

It was generous of Dr. Yalow to speak out for all women at the Nobel Awards ceremony. Do you think it is important for leaders to share the spotlight like this? Write a paragraph or two about what you would do if you received a Nobel Prize.

Ella Fitzgerald

Singer (1918–1996)

Ella Fitzgerald

Ella Fitzgerald, America's "First Lady of Jazz," first thought she wanted to be a dancer.

Ella was born in Newport News, Virginia, on April 25, 1918. But she does not think of herself as a southerner. Shortly after she was born, she moved with her mother and step-father to Yonkers, New York.

Ella's mother had to work as a cook and sometimes managed a laundry to help support her family. But she always had some time left in her day for music. She loved to listen to the radio, and collected records of the singers she liked best. Ella often sat beside her mother as she listened. Soon Ella began to sing along and dance.

Ella was a good student. But sometimes she slipped away from school on afternoons when one of her favorite singers was performing at a theater in her neighborhood. It's not that she did not like school, it's just that she loved music more. She dreamed of someday becoming a performer.

Dancing was what she dreamed about most. One day she entered a talent contest—the Amateur Hour—at the famous Apollo Theater in Harlem, New York City. Ella planned to dance on stage, but once the curtain went up, she froze. Her feet felt like lead. Knowing this audience would not be patient, Ella finally burst into song. She did not feel so awkward singing a popular song, "The Object of My Affection."

This moment was a turning point in Ella's life. The audience loved her. She won first prize, which was a week's work with the theater's great band. At that time the bandleader was the legendary drummer William "Chick" Webb. She said, "I knew right then that I wanted to sing before people for the rest of my life."

She was, of course, a big hit. A pop music critic wrote in his magazine called *Metronome*, "The guys loved her, she loved the guys, and the whole spirit of the band picked up . . . . She was dedicated to her music, never fully ready to recognize her own greatness but forever encouraging the talents of others."

In 1938 she and Chick Webb wrote—and Ella recorded—a "swing" variation on the nursery rhyme "A Tisket, a Tasket." It was Ella's first huge success, and it made Ella a national star.

Chick Webb died in 1939. Ella took up his baton, becoming one of the first female bandleaders in history. Then, when many of the band members were drafted into the army during World War II, Ella did solo acts in nightclubs around the country. She also recorded more songs.

Her mentor was Norman Grantz. She sang in his "Jazz at the Philharmonic" tours in the United States, South America, Asia, and Europe. The crowds were crazy about her kind of music.

Ella fine-tuned a unique singing style called *scat*. Scat (sometimes also called *bebop*) is a wordless musical improvisation. She based this style on the rhythmic patterns of Dizzy Gillespie, a former trumpet player in her band. Gillespie was on his way to becoming one of the greatest trumpet artists in jazz history. Ella's recorded bop versions of "Flyin' Home" and "Lady Be Good" topped sales charts around the world.

She recorded songs from many famous American composers as well. She performed with jazz greats such as Louis Armstrong, Duke Ellington, and Count Basie, to name just three.

For years she toured around the world, tirelessly performing in jazz concerts—often over 40 weeks out of the year. Finally, in 1985, she collapsed from exhaustion. The following year, she had to have quintuple bypass surgery on her heart. She followed doctors' orders and cut the number of performances to two or three a month.

Ella Fitzgerald won many record awards and honors. But she was always quite shy. Asked about her extraordinary talent, and how she created a career with hardly any formal music education, she said, "I've always felt that where I got my education was with the musicians."

She sang for over 60 years and never officially retired. She once said she might retire if it ever got to the point where people didn't want to hear her anymore. But that never happened.

Remembering the Facts

1. Though Ella grew up in Yonkers, New York, she was born where?

2. What kinds of work did Ella's mother do to support her family?

3. What kind of performer did Ella first dream of becoming?

4. What was the name of the famous theater in New York City where Ella entered her first talent contest?

5. What song did Ella sing in her first talent contest?

6. What instrument did the legendary bandleader Chick Webb play?

7. What was the name of Ella's first big hit song?

8. Who took up the baton after Chick Webb died?

9. What is the name of Ella's special kind of jazz?

10. What kind of surgery did Ella have after she collapsed in 1985?

Understanding the Story

1. Ella Fitzgerald was just as popular with other performers as she was with her audience. Why do you think that was so?

2. Music was a very important part of Ella's and her mother's life. Can you understand why?

Getting the Main Idea

Why do you think Ella Fitzgerald would be a good role model for the youth of today?

Applying What You've Learned

Bursting into song was a very brave thing for Ella to do when she "froze" at the talent contest. Write a paragraph telling what you would have done in this situation.

Ruth Bader Ginsberg

Supreme Court Justice
(1933–   )

In 1973 Ruth Bader Ginsberg's daughter, Jane, wrote the following ambition in her high-school yearbook: "To see my mother sit on the U.S. Supreme Court."

Ruth Bader Ginsberg was born on March 15, 1933, in Brooklyn, New York. Her father, a furrier, owned a small store. Her mother was a homemaker.

Ruth Bader Ginsberg

Ruth grew up in a close and loving family. She had one older sister, who sadly died at age six of meningitis. Her parents had not been able to go to college, but they knew how important education was. They encouraged Ruth to work hard for whatever she believed in. They felt that Ruth—or any young girl— should have the same opportunities in life that boys did.

Ruth was number one in her elementary school class. At age 12, she wrote her earliest legal article, "Landmarks of Constitutional Freedom," for the school newspaper.

Cornell University gave Ruth a full scholarship based on her excellent work in high school. Unfortunately, Ruth's mother died of cancer the day before Ruth graduated from high school. But at least she knew before she died that her daughter was going on to college.

Ruth met her future husband, Martin, her first year at Cornell. They were married after graduation in June 1954. Both wanted to become lawyers.

Martin was a year older than Ruth, so he went to Harvard Law School first. His studies were interrupted when he was drafted into the army in 1954. He and Ruth moved to Fort Sill, Oklahoma, where Ruth got an office job.

That job was her first experience with discrimination against women. As soon as her boss leaned she was pregnant, he demoted her. Now more than ever, Ruth wanted to study law.

She decided to apply to Harvard, where Martin would be returning in two years. Everyone except Martin thought she should plan to be a teacher instead. No woman had ever been admitted to Harvard Law School.

But Ruth was determined, so she applied anyway. She was accepted as one of 9 women in a class of more than 500 at Harvard Law School. Life was not easy for these first female law students. There was a great deal of prejudice against them. Even the dean of the law school said, "Do you realize that you are simply taking the place of a qualified man?"

Martin graduated from Harvard in 1958 and took a job in New York City. Ruth wanted her family together, so she changed to Columbia Law School. There she was one of ten women in the class.

She graduated—tied for number one in her class—in 1960. Her first thought was to get a job as a law clerk for a justice of the U.S. Supreme Court. Justice Felix Frankfurter turned her down immediately, saying, "I don't hire women."

It was the first of many rejections for Ruth. Even though she was tops in her class, no one would hire her. They would not hire her first because she was a woman, second because she was Jewish, and third because she was a mother. At this time there was still prejudice against Jews. And employers thought mothers couldn't possibly have jobs and also care for their children.

Finally Ruth got a job as a legal secretary. Then, in 1963 she was hired by Rutgers School of Law in New Jersey as a professor. She was one of the first 20 women ever hired to teach in an American law school.

When she became pregnant with her second child, Ruth wore baggy clothes so no one could tell. She did not want to be demoted again. Fortunately, her son was born during the summer. She could return to teaching in time for fall classes.

At Rutgers, Ruth discovered that women professors were paid less than men for the same work. She got this policy changed, then went on to argue several other cases on behalf of women. Not surprisingly, one of the first rules she changed was the one that forced women to quit their jobs when they became pregnant. Ruth taught at Rutgers for nine years before she was hired by Columbia Law School as its first female law professor.

In 1980 President Jimmy Carter appointed Ruth to the U.S. Court of Appeals, the second highest court in the United States. There she was known for "being tough on crime, committed to free speech and freedom of religion, and supportive of civil rights." Then, in 1993, President Bill Clinton chose her for the Supreme Court.

In his historic announcement, President Clinton said, "Ruth Bader Ginsberg is one of the nation's best judges. Throughout her life she has repeatedly stood for the individual, the person less well-off, the outside in society, and has given these people greater hope by telling them they have a place in our legal system."

Jane's high-school yearbook wish had come true.

Remembering the Facts

1. Where did Ruth's daughter, Jane, write that she wanted to see her mother on the Supreme Court?

2. How many years passed before Jane's wish came true?

3. How old was Ruth when she wrote her first legal article?

4. Which university awarded Ruth a full scholarship?

5. What caused her mother to die?

6. Where did Ruth and Martin live after he was drafted into the army?

7. Why was Ruth Bader Ginsberg demoted in her office job?

8. Which Supreme Court Justice told Ruth, "I don't hire women"?

9. What was the name of the first law school to hire Ruth Bader Ginsberg to teach?

10. Which president chose Ruth Bader Ginsberg for the Supreme Court?

Understanding the Story

1. Ruth Bader Ginsberg experienced much prejudice against women. How do you think that affected her legal decisions?

2. Where did Ruth get support for her career choices?

Getting the Main Idea

Why do you think Ruth Bader Ginsberg would be a good role model for young people today?

Applying What You've Learned

Even though Ruth Bader Ginsberg experienced much prejudice, she never became bitter or lost her sense of fairness. If you had to work against the same biases, do you think you could remain so open-minded?

Ka'iulani of Hawaii

An "American" Princess
(1875–1899)

We do not think of the United States as having kings or queens, princes or princesses, or royal families. But once, briefly, we did have a real princess — Ka'iulani of Hawaii.

The island kingdom celebrated when Ka'iulani was born on October 16, 1875. Her granduncle, King Kalakaua, had no children, so he named his sister, Lilinokalani, heir to the Hawaiian throne. Next in line of succession was her daughter, Princess Like-like. Ka'iulani was the only child of Princess Likelike and Archibald Cleghorn, a man from Scotland who ran a prosperous business in Hawaii. The people were overjoyed about this newest member of their royal family.

Ka'iulani of Hawaii

The princess's full name was Princess Victoria Ka'iulani, Kalaninuiahilapalapa Kawekiu i Lunalilo. Ka'iulani means "the royal sacred one." Her father was a friend and adviser to the king. He was also an expert in growing plants and flowers, so the grounds around the princess's house were some of the most beautiful on the islands.

There were giant turtles and peacocks to entertain Ka'iulani, but she was not at all spoiled. People loved her. She was an expert horsewoman, surfer, and swimmer. She even dared to go beyond reefs where some men wouldn't go.

She was very happy until her mother died. Ka'iulani was 11 years old at the time. Her father decided it was time to send her to school in England. "Only there," he said, "can you receive an education fit for a queen."

Ka'iulani tried to be very brave. It would be hard for her to leave her father, her family and friends, and her beautiful house and gardens. Another Scotsman, Robert Louis Stevenson (author of *Treasure Island* and *Kidnapped*), happened to be visiting Hawaii at this time. He spoke to Princess Ka'iulani about England and eased some of her fears.

Her father sailed with her as far as San Francisco. Then she took a train across the United States and boarded another ship to cross the Atlantic Ocean.

She was happy once she finally arrived in England. The ocean voyage had been long, and she was seasick most of the time. Ka'iulani loved school. She made new friends there. And she looked forward to being presented at the English court to her namesake, Queen Victoria.

Over time, however, letters from home filled her heart with sadness. Slowly but surely, groups of American businessmen tried to take control of Hawaii. They called the native Hawaiians savages, and said the natives should be grateful for the Americans' business expertise.

The Americans wanted to annex Hawaii to the United States. King Kalakana died trying to stop them. His sister became Queen Lilinokalani. She named Princess Ka'iulani next in line for the throne.

But it wasn't long before American businessmen forced Queen Lilinokalani off the throne and set up their own government.

Princess Ka'iulani did not know how to help her people. Friends suggested she speak directly to the American president, Grover Cleveland. If she could persuade him of the injustice, Cleveland could block the annexation.

"What can I do to influence one of the greatest nations on earth?" Ka'iulani asked. "I'm only a 17-year-old student." But she could not let her people down. She had to try to meet with President Cleveland.

A few weeks later, Ka'iulani set sail for the United States. She explained her mission to news reporters before leaving England, and then again when she arrived in America. The public was thrilled to read about this young princess's courage.

President Cleveland, too, was impressed by this brave princess. He agreed to try to stop the annexation and to give the royal family their throne again.

Unfortunately, he was powerless against the Americans who had taken over Hawaii. The only way Cleveland could have stopped them was to send in the army. He refused to do that. All he could do was block the annexation as long as he was president.

Ka'iulani went home to offer what help she could to her people. Things were very different from when she had left for school not so very long ago. Her beautiful gardens were overgrown with weeds. The people were sad.

Shortly after President Cleveland left office in 1897, Congress voted to annex Hawaii to the United States. Hawaii was no longer an independent nation. Ka'iulani and her people wept as the Americans celebrated. The young princess worked hard trying to keep peace among her people. Sometimes it worked, but more often it was a losing battle. Even she could not give back her people's good spirit, their love of life.

In March of 1899, Princess Ka'iulani died at the age of 24. Some said it was from rheumatism. Others said it was from despair. The Hawaiian people were overwhelmed with sadness. Thousands attended her funeral. This princess never lived to become a queen.

Remembering the Facts

1. When was Princess Ka'iulani born?

2. How was King Kalakaua related to the princess?

3. What did Princess Ka'iulani's name mean?

4. What was the name of Ka'iulani's mother?

5. What country was the princess's father from?

6. What are two kinds of animals that entertained Princess Ka'iulani as a child?

7. How old was the princess when her mother died?

8. What was the name of the author of *Treasure Island* and *Kidnapped* who visited Hawaii?

9. How far did her father sail with the princess when she went away to school?

10. Who was president of the United States at this time?

Understanding the Story

1. Where did Princess Ka'iulani's father want to send her to school? Why do you think he selected this country?

2. Why do you think the Hawaiians were sad when their country was annexed by the United States?

Getting the Main Idea

Why do you think Princess Ka'iulani would be a good role model for young people today?

Applying What You've Learned

Princess Ka'iulani was brave and she cared about her people. Write a paragraph explaining why you think any leader should have these two important traits.

Barbara Jordan

Congresswoman (1936–1996)

Barbara Jordan had a brilliant political career. Perhaps the moment for which she is best remembered happened in 1974, during the impeachment hearings for President Richard M. Nixon after his Watergate scandal. Jordan was on the House Judiciary Committee, charged with judging the evidence against President Nixon.

Barbara Jordan

Jordan's powerful opening remarks moved not only her fellow committee members, but also the world at large who watched the hearings on television. She said, "When the U.S. Constitution was completed on the seventeenth of September in 1787, I was not included in that 'We, the people.' I felt somehow for many years that George Washington and Alexander Hamilton just left me out by mistake. But through the process of amendment, interpretation, and court decisions, I have finally been included . . . And I am not going to sit here and be an idle spectator to the destruction of the Constitution."

She argued that the evidence against Nixon was so powerful that if the committee did not vote for impeachment, "then perhaps the eighteenth-century Constitution should be abandoned to the twentieth-century paper shredder."

Jordan had been elected to the U.S. Congress just two years earlier. Before this she had served six years in the Texas State Senate—the first African-American senator in Texas since 1883.

Barbara Charline Jordan was born in Houston, Texas, in 1936. She had two older sisters, both of whom became music teachers. Her father was a Baptist minister and her mother was a domestic worker. "We were poor," Jordan said, "but so was everyone else around us, so we didn't really notice. Besides, we were never hungry and we always had a place to stay."

In high school, Jordan won first prizes for her speeches in national oratory contests. Then, at the all-black college she attended in Houston, she led the debating team to a series of championships.

Still, this was before the 1964 Civil Rights movement. Jordan saw many injustices against her people. She decided to study law to see if there was anything she could do to change the system. She got her law degree from Boston University, where she says she experienced more prejudice because she was a woman than because she was an African American.

After graduation Barbara Jordan went back home to Texas and lived with her parents. She used their dining-room table as her law office until she could afford space of her own.

In 1960 Jordan was a volunteer for John F. Kennedy's presidential campaign. She began licking stamps and stuffing envelopes, but ended up working to get a record number of African Americans out to help elect Kennedy.

Barbara Jordan began to think that politics might be the way for her to bring about change. She ran for the Texas House of Representatives two times and lost. Then, she ran for the Texas Senate in 1966 and won.

She served in the Texas Senate for the next six years. She worked hard to pass antidiscrimination laws and to set up a minimum working wage. Jordan managed to get half of the bills she introduced passed into laws. This is an extraordinary record for any senator, no matter what race or gender.

In 1972 she was elected to the United States House of Representatives. There she kept fighting to end discrimination. She also worked for more aid to schools, legal aid for the poor, environmental protection laws, and workmen's compensation. And she tried to limit U.S. involvement in Vietnam.

After her great Watergate speech before the House Judiciary Committee in 1974, Jordan was asked to give the keynote address at the Democratic National Convention. People were stunned when, in 1977, she announced that she would not run for a fourth term in Congress. Though she did not like to admit it, she had a neuromuscular problem that kept her in a wheelchair.

Jordan was elected to the Orators Hall of Fame and the National Women's Hall of Fame in Seneca Falls, New York. She was named "Best Living Orator" by the International (Debating) Platform Association. Always working to get better lives for black people and others who are in need, she had changed many laws to help them.

Later she became a professor at the Lyndon B. Johnson School of Public Affairs at the University of Texas in Austin.

Jordan believed that Texas was more than just a state. She spoke of it as a frame of mind. She said, "I believe that I get from the soil and the spirit of Texas the feeling that I, as an individual, can accomplish whatever I want to and that there are no limits . . . . I like that spirit."

She told young people that if they are not satisfied, they should find jobs in government and make decisions: "Do the job and make it work for you." She did it—so she knew it could be done!

Remembering the Facts

1. What did Barbara Jordan do at the University of Texas?

2. The 1974 impeachment hearings were being held for which president of the United States?

3. What was the committee Jordan was serving on when she made her famous speech about the Constitution?

4. What did Jordan say they should do with the Constitution if the committee did not vote for impeachment?

5. What international association named Jordan "Best Living Orator"?

6. Jordan was the first African-American senator in Texas since when?

7. Where was Jordan born?

8. Did Jordan win or lose when she was running for the Texas House of Representatives?

9. Where did Jordan get her law degree?

10. What kind of discrimination did Jordan experience in law school?

Understanding the Story

1. What did Jordan feel was so special about Texas?

2. Jordan's family was poor when she was growing up, but she never felt poor. Do you know why?

Getting the Main Idea

Why do you think Barbara Jordan would be a good role model for young people today?

Applying What You've Learned

Even though Barbara Jordan was born poor and black, she felt she could do whatever she wanted in life. Can you think of some injustices in your school, community, or home today that you would like to correct? Write a paragraph or two to describe the problem as you see it. Tell what you think you could do to improve the situation.

Donna Karan

Fashion Designer (1948–   )

The newspapers called Donna Karan "Queen of Seventh Avenue." Seventh Avenue is the heart of the fashion design district in New York City. In fact, it is the heart of American fashion. Donna's huge success in the competitive world of fashion design is based on her philosophy: "I want to give the woman her own personal style so that her personality supersedes the clothes so that she and her own feelings come through . . ."

Donna Karan

Asked how she came to be so successful, Donna said, "Fashion is something that's in your blood." It's always been part of Donna's life. Donna was born in Forest Hills, New York, in 1948. Her mother, Helen, was a model. Her father, Gabby, was a well-known tailor in New York City. He often created clothes for celebrities.

Donna's father was killed in an automobile accident when she was three years old. "Sometimes," Donna says, "I feel my mother left me then too." Her mother had to work to support Donna and her older sister. Donna resented that her mother did not have more time to spend with her family.

Donna was not very popular in school. Her nicknames were "Popeye" and "Spaghetti Legs." She liked sports in school, but not many of her classes except art. In school she created her first fashion collection by tracing patterns around her own body.

One summer she pretended to be older than 14 to get a job in a small clothing store. She loved her work. It gave her "a sense of what people looked good in and what they didn't."

In 1966 Donna was accepted at the Parsons School of Design in New York City. She got in not so much for her grades, which were not great, but on the recommendation of the designer her mother worked for.

At Parsons, she met Louis Dell'Olio. With him she would share a long-term business partnership. She said, "I would sew his clothes and he would draw mine."

She applied at Anne Klein's fashion design house for a summer intern job when she was just 16. In the 1960's and 1970's, Anne made popular sports clothes for women—clothes that women could feel comfortable working and moving in. Anne liked Donna's work so much that she took her on permanently. (Donna did not get back to Parsons for her degree until 1987.)

At the time, however, Donna was also in love with Mark Karan. He owned a clothing boutique in Miami Beach, Florida. Donna decided to marry Mark because "fashion was not going to be the only thing in life that would be important to me." They had a daughter they named Gabby after Donna's father. The marriage lasted ten years. Later Donna married Stephan Weiss, a sculptor.

Gabby was born just days before Anne Klein died of cancer. Donna said, "I could not believe Anne could do this to me. Along with the sorrow [of her death] I was angry because I had no time for this. I was a new mother."

But the business had to go on. When Donna could not get into the office, employees trucked the clothes and themselves to Donna's house. Finally, Donna gave up and returned to the office. Then she was made chief designer.

In May—less than six weeks after Anne Klein had died—Donna presented her first collection as chief designer. It seemed like a miracle, and it was a smash hit. The audience gave her a standing ovation—for her designs as well as her superhuman effort to get the collection out on time.

The next year, Donna made Dell'Olio her design partner. Together, in 10 years, they built the company from a $10 million into a $75 million business—a stunning success.

In 1985 Donna created her own company called Donna Karan New York. Her first collection, and every one since, has won high praise from fashion critics. One said, "She's the only female world-class designer in the United States."

Donna never creates any clothing that she would not wear herself. She said, "I'm a working woman. I need to make my life easier. I don't have time to spend hours selecting outfits to wear each day." She wants her clothes to reflect real life.

Donna identified the key pieces of any woman's wardrobe. From this she created a system in which each piece (skirt, pants, blouse, jacket) was interchangeable. The clothes did not go out of style quickly. A woman could wear her favorites until they fell apart. No one had to buy whole new outfits every season.

She designed soft and sophisticated clothing for high-powered women. Donna said to a reporter, "I love freedom of body movement and modern jazz and I've always wanted to get that ease and motion into clothes."

In 1988 Donna launched a new line of clothes called DKNY. This is a less expensive collection for women who want to look fashionable but cannot afford the price of custom-designed clothing.

Four years later she launched a collection for men. A lot of people thought men would not buy clothes with a woman designer's name on them, but they were wrong. President Bill Clinton is one of her best customers!

Donna's collections are now sold in over 300 of the best clothing stores in the United States. Some of the biggest names in the world of professional women—Diane Sawyer, Barbara Walters, Barbra Streisand, and Candice Bergen on her TV show *Murphy Brown*—wear Donna's fashions.

Donna was named Designer of the Year by the Council of Fashion Designers of America in 1985. Then, in 1992, the same council named her Men's Designer of the Year. But Donna never sits back to rest on last year's praise. "I have to reinvent myself every season," she says. Donna Karan's fashions are not just about clothes. They are more about people—how to make people feel good about themselves so they can make a difference in their lives and the lives of others.

Remembering the Facts

1. Donna Karan was named queen of what avenue?

2. What did Donna's mother do in the fashion business?

3. What did Donna's father do in the fashion business?

4. What was one of the nicknames Donna's schoolmates called her?

5. What is the name of the famous school of design that Donna attended in New York?

6. What was the name of the woman designer who gave Donna her first job?

7. Who did Donna name after her father, Gabby?

8. What kind of artist was Donna's second husband?

9. Which U.S. president likes to wear Donna's fashions?

10. What award did the Council of Fashion Designers bestow on Donna in 1985?

Understanding the Story

1. Why do you think family is so important to Donna?

2. Why was it so important for Donna to make stylish clothes comfortable for women?

Getting the Main Idea

Why do you think Donna Karan would be a good role model for young people today?

Applying What You've Learned

If you were designing clothes for today's busy women, what kind of wardrobe would you create?

Elizabeth Cochrane Seaman (Nellie Bly)

Journalist (1867–1922)

Elizabeth Cochrane— later and better known as "Nellie Bly"—was born in Cochran's Mills, a small town near Pittsburgh, Pennsylvania. The town was named after her father, Michael Cochrane.

Other Cochran's Mills mothers dressed their daughters in practical shades of gray and brown. Elizabeth's mother, however, chose bright pink outfits for her little girl. So she was nicknamed Pink. A recent biographer named Brooke Kroeger wrote, "From the very start, Mrs. Cochrane groomed her daughter to know how to attract attention and to revel in it. The lessons would never be lost."

Elizabeth Cochrane Seaman

Elizabeth grew up with nine brothers and sisters. She went to the public school down the street from their house. Her father died when Elizabeth was about eight years old. Elizabeth's mother remarried. However, they ended up divorcing—something very unusual in those days.

Elizabeth wanted to go on to college and become a teacher. She enrolled at the local college. But she had to drop out after her first year due to lack of family money.

Elizabeth got her first taste of journalism at the age of 20. She moved to join her mother in Pittsburgh after leaving college. In 1885, the *Pittsburgh Dispatch* published an editorial called "What Girls Are Good For." The article was against women's suffrage. Outraged, Elizabeth fired off a letter to the editor of the paper. She signed it "The Lonely Orphan Girl." She provided no return address.

The editor was so taken with Elizabeth's writing that he placed an ad in his paper to find her. "If the 'Lonely Orphan Girl' will send her name and address to this office . . . , she will confer a favor and receive the information she desires."

The next day Elizabeth arrived at the editor's office in person. He asked her to write an answer to his column, and she did. Her article, "The Girl Puzzle," was published on the first page of the Sunday paper. It spoke on behalf of working women in Pittsburgh, and it was a great hit. Soon Elizabeth become a regular reporter for the *Pittsburgh Dispatch*.

Writing for a newspaper—especially writing the stories Elizabeth wanted to write—was not considered "ladylike" then. So women reporters always signed their columns with a pseudonym (a made-up name). Elizabeth chose to write under the name Nellie Bly, from the song by Stephen Foster.

Nellie did not just write about women's suffrage. She also reported on poor working conditions in local factories, the problems of a working girl, slums, and even divorce (which was rarely discussed in public).

The *Dispatch* soon sent Nellie to Mexico to write about the horrible contrast between the lives of the very rich and the very poor. She also wrote about Mexican politics—their corruption and need for reform. Nellie's articles were so powerful that the Mexican government finally made her leave to stop the negative news about Mexico.

Nellie returned to the United States in 1887. She went to Joseph Pulitzer's paper, the *World*, in New York City. She persuaded the famous newsman to let her report on the dreadful brutality and neglect suffered by mentally ill patients. She pretended to be insane so she could be admitted to the public asylum on Blackwell's Island. Nellie's reports from inside the asylum shocked the world. They helped finally to bring about many reforms in care for the mentally ill.

From then on Nellie chose many different disguises. She worked in a sweatshop; she had herself arrested to see what happened to a woman in jail; she danced in a corps de ballet. Whenever she saw an injustice, she jumped right in to investigate. Then she exposed the culprits in print.

Delighted with her success, Pulitzer organized a trip around the world in 1889. Nellie was going to try to beat the record set in Jules Verne's novel *Around the World in Eighty Days*. Nellie made the journey in 72 days, 6 hours and 11 minutes. Her only luggage was a single bag 16 inches long and 7 inches tall! The newspaper published daily accounts of her trip on its front page. Nellie Bly became a sensation. It was the highlight of her career.

In 1895, Nellie was on a train to New York from the Midwest. She had been reporting on drought and forest fires. She met a wealthy businessman named Robert Seaman on the train. They were married a few days later. He was 72; Nellie was 28. They seemed happy, although he only lived for nine more years.

After his death, Nellie went to Europe. She sent letters back to the *World* about the problems there. Several years later, those problems resulted in World War I.

After the war, Nellie returned to the United States and a new job at the *New York Journal*. Older and tired now, she did not report on the more unpopular causes. She is most often remembered for her sensational trip around the world. But Nellie Bly was also one of the earliest reporters to expose some of the great injustices in this world.

At the time of her death in 1922, the *New York Evening Journal* wrote, "Nellie Bly was the best reporter in America."

Remembering the Facts

1. What was Nellie Bly's real name?

2. Who was the famous composer who wrote a song about Nellie Bly?

3. What was Nellie's childhood nickname?

4. Why did Nellie want to go to college?

5. What was the name of Nellie's first newspaper?

6. What was the title of the editorial that infuriated Nellie?

7. How did Nellie sign her letter to the editor?

8. What was the title of Nellie's first article for the *Dispatch*?

9. Who was the author of the book *Around the World in Eighty Days*?

10. Where was the mental institution where Nellie admitted herself to expose the terrible conditions?

Understanding the Story

1. Nellie took the time to write about many injustices in this world. Do you think, as some people did, that she did it only to draw attention to herself?

2. Nellie had wanted to become a teacher. Do you think she taught through her writing?

Getting the Main Idea

Why do you think Nellie Bly is a good role model for young people today?

Applying What You've Learned

If you saw a situation where people were being treated unfairly, how would you try to correct it?

Nikki Giovanni

Poet (1943–)

Nikki Giovanni's first book, *Black Feeling, Black Talk*, was published in 1967. Since then, her poems have moved people, have opened new doors in their lives.

Nikki was born in Knoxville, Tennessee, in 1943. Her given name was Yolande Cornelia Giovanni, Jr. Several months later she and her parents and her older sister, Gary, moved to Cincinnati, Ohio.

The Giovannis were poor, but Nikki says their life was good. They may not have had indoor plumbing, but they had hundreds of books and a piano in their modest house.

Nikki Giovanni

Her father struggled to improve the family's living conditions. But the emotional cost on the family was high. Nikki couldn't bear to see her parents arguing so much. The summer before she was to enter high school, she called her grandmother, Louvenia, in Knoxville. She asked if she could come for a visit. Then, once Nikki was there, she asked her grandparents if she could stay. And she did—for three years!

Nikki helped not only with household chores but also with Louvenia's social, political, and charitable activities. When African

Americans were needed in town to demonstrate against racial injustices, Louvenia sent Nikki. When someone was needed to help carry food to sick or shut-in neighbors, Louvenia volunteered Nikki. Nikki developed a strong sense of responsibility for her family and for her black community. Nikki calls the lesson "a strong sense of giving something back."

Another person who had a great influence on Nikki's life at this time was Miss Alfreda Delaney, her high-school English teacher. Miss Delaney encouraged Nikki to read African-American authors, and to write about what she had read. For the first time Nikki learned that a writer *could* make a difference.

Being a very bright student, Nikki entered Fisk University when she was just 17. Here, however, her feisty independence got in her way. She was in constant conflict with the dean of women. When Nikki left campus to go to Thanksgiving dinner at her grandparents' house without asking permission, the dean dismissed her from school.

It was three years before Nikki returned to Fisk. But then Fisk had a new dean of women who supported Nikki's writing and political activities. Nikki set up a chapter of SNCC (Student Nonviolent Coordinating Committee) on campus. She got involved in the black arts movement and also edited a student literary journal.

Nikki's grandmother, Louvenia, died just two months after Nikki's graduation in 1966. Nikki moved back to Cincinnati and tried to write her way through her grief. Within a year, she had finished a collection of poems for her first book. She also organized Cincinnati's first Black Arts Festival. "A festival celebrating black art and artists was always to remain her concept of revolution . . . ." Nikki believes in the power of the individual, whether the person is a gifted artist or an ordinary, caring human being. She has said that "White racists control blacks by lumping them all together and refusing to recognize them as individuals." She believes that "progress at the cost of human lives is no progress at all."

By the end of 1968 Nikki had completed most of the poems for her second book, *Black Judgment.* She moved to New York City to enroll in the School of Fine Arts at Columbia University. When her Columbia professors said she couldn't write, she left their program and published her book, *Black Feeling/Black Talk*. Critics loved the book. Nikki never again had to prove that she could write.

In 1969 Nikki returned to Cincinnati. She gave birth to her only child, Thomas Watson Giovanni. Then she and the baby moved to New Jersey, where Nikki taught at Rutgers University.

Next Nikki edited a collection of poetry, *Night Comes Softly*. It was one of the first anthologies of poetry by African-American women.

In the first 10 years of her writing career, Nikki published 12 books. She also released five record albums. One of them, *Truth Is on Its Way*, was a best-seller; it received a national award for the best spoken book of the year.

Nikki was, and is, enormously popular. Knowing that many people do not read poetry books, Nikki took her words "on the road." All during the 1970's Nikki spoke in cities, towns, churches, Y's, and bookstores throughout the United States and around the world. Wherever people would stop and listen, she spoke. And she always took Thomas with her.

Nikki believes in the power of poetry to bring about change. She says, "Always poems are written because . . . the heart explodes with the necessity to bare itself in the hope that others might see . . . Poetry can define the life or lack of life that we are leading."

Her work is a celebration of African-American life. One of her most famous poems is "Black Love Is Black Wealth." Today she has written over 17 books and published dozens of individual poems and articles. In 1994 alone, Nikki published four new books. One is a picture-book edition of her poem "Knoxville Tennessee." It is a magnificent book, celebrating in words and pictures a loving homecoming in Knoxville.

Nikki Giovanni speaks with eloquence and joy on behalf of her people and on behalf of all people. We would do well to listen to this extraordinary American woman's revolutionary words.

Remembering the Facts

1. What is Nikki Giovanni's given name?

2. What is the name of Nikki Giovanni's first book?

3. Where was Nikki born?

4. What was the name of Nikki's grandmother?

5. Miss Alfreda Delaney taught what subject in Nikki's high school?

6. From what university did Nikki graduate?

7. What does SNCC stand for?

8. What is the name of the collection of poetry by African-American women that Nikki edited?

9. What is the name of Nikki best-selling record album?

10. What is the name of Nikki Giovanni's famous poem that talks about black love?

Understanding the Story

1. Why did Nikki not think her family was poor?

2. Who were the most important people in Nikki's life?

Getting the Main Idea

Why do you think Nikki Giovanni would be a good role model for young people today?

Applying What You've Learned

Write a short paragraph to describe how you think Nikki has lived up to her grandmother's lessons about the importance of giving something back to your family and your community.

Bonnie Blair

Speed Skater (1964–)

Speed skater Bonnie Blair has won five Olympic gold medals—more than any other American woman. She won her first in the 1988 Winter Olympics in Calgary, Canada; two more at the 1992 Winter Games in Albertville, France; and another two at the 1994 Winter Olympics in Lillehammer, Norway.

Bonnie Blair

Bonnie Kathleen Blair was born on March 18, 1964, in Cornwall, New York. She had five older brothers and sisters. A favorite family story is that on the day Bonnie was born, her father was supposed to work as a timer at a skating meet. Several other Blair children were racing there. He did not want to miss the meet, and he knew it might be a long wait at the hospital. So Mr. Blair dropped Bonnie's mother off and went on to the skating rink. During the meet, the announcer's voice interrupted the events just long enough to say, "Looks like the Blairs have another skater!" That was Bonnie's first "appearance" at a skating rink.

All the Blair children were interested in speed skating. The fancy moves involved in figure skating did not interest them. Later, their mother said, "All Bonnie ever wanted out of skating was to skate and create the wind around her."

Bonnie's family moved to Champaign, Illinois, when she was two years old. By the time she was three, she was taking her first skating steps. Five of her older brothers and sisters were great skaters; almost as soon as Bonnie could stand up and walk, they took her to the ice rink. Her feet were so tiny they had to put a pair of skates on over her shoes, but Bonnie remembers those first steps on the ice more clearly than walking.

Bonnie entered her first official race at age four. When she was six she was beating girls much older, and at seven she skated in the Illinois State Championships.

In 1979, when she was 15, Bonnie made it to the United States Olympic trials. She just barely missed making the team for the 1980 Olympics in Lake Placid, New York.

Her coach advised her to go to Europe to train for the 1984 Olympics. Bonnie's family could not afford to send her there. So Bonnie raised the money ($7000) on her own. And while she was in Europe she completed her high-school degree by mail.

She made the 1984 Olympic Team and competed at Sarajevo, Yugoslavia. But it would be four more years—at the Winter Games in Calgary—before she won her first gold medal. The event was the 500-meter race. Bonnie beat her opponent by just two-hundredths of a second—or less than 1 foot. She also won a bronze medal that year in the 1000-meter event. Bonnie was the only U.S. athlete to win two medals, so her teammates asked her to carry the American flag in the closing ceremonies.

Bonnie won two more gold medals at Lillehammer, Norway (again in the 500- and 1000-meter races). She had won more gold medals than any other American woman in Olympian history. Experts agree she is one of the greatest technical speed skaters in the world. Still, it's not winning, but the race itself, that Bonnie loves. She entered an extra race—the 1500-meter—in her free time at Lillehammer just "for the thrill of competition."

Whenever possible, Bonnie's family and friends go to the competitions with her. Twenty-five of them cheered her on in Norway. Her older brothers and sisters have no regrets about not achieving the same fame as Bonnie. They are very proud of their little sister.

Sports Illustrated named Bonnie Blair "Sportswoman of the Year" in 1994—not only because of her Olympic medals, but also because she is such a great human being.

Remembering the Facts

1. How many Olympic gold medals has Bonnie Blair won?

2. Where did Bonnie win her first Olympic gold medal?

3. Why didn't the Blairs like figure skating?

4. How old was Bonnie the first time she skated?

5. Where was Bonnie born?

6. What happened when Bonnie's family did not have enough money to send Bonnie to Europe to train for the 1984 Olympics?

7. Where was Bonnie's father when she was born?

8. Bonnie won her first gold medal by two-hundredths of a second in what speed skating event?

9. For which Olympics did Bonnie carry the American flag in the closing ceremonies?

10. Which magazine named Bonnie "Sportswoman of the Year" in 1994?

Understanding the Story

1. Bonnie loves to skate, and not just for the gold. What do you think she likes best about this sport?

2. Do you think Bonnie is distracted or encouraged by the numbers of family and friends who show up at her competitions?

Getting the Main Idea

Why do you think Bonnie Blair would be a good role model for young people today?

Applying What You've Learned

Participating in Olympic events carries a tremendous amount of pressure as well as excitement. How would you feel if you were chosen to represent your country in an Olympic event?

Key Vocabulary

Helen Keller

advocate	indicate	achievement
siege	possibility	autobiography
communicate	discipline	lobbied
destructive	meaningless	honorary
mimic		

Eleanor Roosevelt

humanitarian	gala	migrant
remarkable	politicians	sharecroppers
mottoes	campaign	racial
instill	paralyzed	injustice
diphtheria	lectures	delegation
exhausted	hostess	document
investigated		

Georgia O'Keeffe

classic	post-Impressionist	express
attracted	sketches	delicate
recognize	art gallery	inspire
encouraged	creativity	unique
appreciate	stifled	ordinary

Julia Morgan

trailblazing	tradition	structure
architecture	determined	Spanish revival
wealth	financing	anonymously
inherited	commissions	compound
opportunities	recommendations	monasteries
excel	established	

Wilma P. Mankiller

chief	rural	lobbied
honorary	union activist	heritage
ancestors	demonstrators	self-esteem
fertile	coordinator	rehabilitation
relocation	campaigned	muscular dystrophy
drought		

Rachel Carson

dedicated	toxic	ecology
conservationist	destiny	topography
chemical pesticides	solitary	origins
environment	fascinated	controversy
uproar	imagination	investigate
sponsor	zoology	chronicle

Dorothea Lange

immigrants	assignment	drifter
tenement	studio	longshoremen
polio	reputation	migrant
portrait	interfere	reveal
apprentice	luxuries	

Rosalyn Sussman Yalow

dynamite
establish
annual
benefit
enzymes
detect

insulin
diabetics
radioscope
tracers
twine
physics

handicap
appointed
physicist
aspirations
competence
responsibility

Ella Fitzgerald

performer
amateur
bandleader
legendary
recognize

encouraging
mentor
Philharmonic
fine-tuned
improvisation

rhythmic
jazz
bop
composer
quintuple bypass

Ruth Bader Ginsberg

ambition
furrier
homemaker
meningitis
opportunities
article

constitutional
scholarship
interrupted
discrimination
demoted

prejudice
rejections
policy
behalf
committed

Ka'iulani of Hawaii

kingdom
heir
succession
prosperous
voyage
namesake

savages
expertise
annex
persuade
injustice
influence

mission
powerless
rheumatism
despair
overwhelmed

Barbara Jordan

brilliant	spectator	prejudice
career	celebrities	campaign
impeachment	resented	antidiscrimination
scandal	historic	involvement
judiciary	domestic	keynote
evidence	oratory	neuromuscular
amendment	injustices	

Donna Karan

fashion design	recommendation	misgivings
competitive	partnership	ovation
philosophy	permanently	wardrobe
design	boutique	interchangeable
personality	sculptor	launched
supersedes		

Elizabeth Cochrane Seaman (Nellie Bly)

practical	outraged	brutality
recent	editor	neglect
biographer	confer	asylum
groomed	column	disguise
revel	behalf	corps de ballet
journalism	slums	culprits
editorial	contrast	sensation
suffrage	corruption	drought

Nikki Giovanni

modest	feisty	festival
emotional	campus	anthologies
charitable	literary	eloquence
demonstrate	conflict	revolutionary
shut-in		

Bonnie Blair

rink	afford	technical
appearance	competed	competition
official	opponent	achieving
championships	ceremonies	

Answers

HELEN KELLER

Remembering the Facts

1. Tuscumbia, Alabama
2. Siege of Vicksburg
3. 19 months old
4. Charles Dickens
5. Laura Bridgeman

6. Because his wife was deaf
7. Annie M. Sullivan
8. Water
9. Square hand
10. Radcliffe College

Understanding the Story

(Answers may vary)

1. Helen learned to create hand signals for the things she wanted.
2. Her mother and Alexander Graham Bell

Getting the Main Idea

This is an inspiring story about how one individual can overcome seemingly insurmountable obstacles to lead a rich and full life.

Applying What You've Learned

You should try to communicate through senses other than your eyes and ears.

ELEANOR ROOSEVELT

Remembering the Facts

1. Fear of drowning
2. Two brothers—one of whom died of diphtheria before he was two years old.
3. Diphtheria
4. Allenswood
5. New York State senator
6. Washington, DC
7. Polio
8. 1932
9. He asked Eleanor to join the U.S. delegation to the first General Assembly of the United Nations.
10. John F. Kennedy

Understanding the Story

(Answers may vary)

1. No; she felt unloved by her mother, and both of her parents died when she was very young.
2. Eleanor was a compassionate human being. She saw a lot of human suffering acting as the "President's eyes," and she tried to correct injustice wherever she could.

Getting the Main Idea

Eleanor was loyal to her husband and she was loyal to the people. She was willing to take a stand (even if it was an unpopular one) to eliminate racial prejudice and social injustice.

Applying What You've Learned

You should include an explanation of how you would gather accurate information about the people, some ideas for eliminating poverty and prejudice, and what you think you'd need to do to bring about change.

GEORGIA O'KEEFFE

Remembering the Facts

1. Flowers, bones, clouds, and mountains
2. Sun Prairie
3. Red rose
4. Her school principal
5. William Merritt Chase
6. She learned how colors and shapes can have lives of their own.
7. Columbia Teachers College in New York City
8. Charcoal
9. He was a photographer.
10. Abiquiu

Understanding the Story

(Answers may vary)

1. The principal of her school encouraged Georgia to paint whatever she wanted, instead of forcing her to do class assignments, and told her mother that Georgia should go to art school. Georgia's mother agreed and enrolled her at the Art Students League.
2. It brought her closer to nature—the flowers, bones, mountains, and clouds that she painted all her life.

Getting the Main Idea

Georgia had the courage to stick with what she wanted to do (be an artist) instead of doing what society thought women should do (be an art teacher).

Applying What You've Learned

You should explain how it takes a great deal of courage to go against others' expectations, to be who you want to be.

JULIA MORGAN

Remembering the Facts

1. San Francisco, California
2. She worked out on her brother's gym equipment.
3. Pierre LeBrun
4. École des Beaux Arts
5. Newspaper
6. To rebuild the elegant Fairmont Hotel
7. Red shingles
8. 20
9. Nearly one third
10. Over 800

Understanding the Story

(Answers may vary)

1. Because Julia suffered so much prejudice against women when she was a student
2. Her use of natural products such as red shingles whenever possible

Getting the Main Idea

You should mention Julia Morgan's taking up a profession new to women, the obstacles she had to overcome, and how she went on to help other women overcome those same obstacles.

Applying What You've Learned

You should talk about how it feels to be singled out and how it feels to be considered less than equal to others.

WILMA P. MANKILLER

Remembering the Facts

1. Navajo
2. Oklahoma
3. 160 acres
4. Trail of Tears
5. San Francisco
6. Ecuador
7. Alcatraz
8. Ross Swimmer
9. *Ms.* magazine
10. Muscular dystrophy

Understanding the Story

(Answers may vary)

1. Because they were driven out of their homeland by the U.S. government
2. Wilma has had to deal with her people's lack of interest in their own welfare, a horrible automobile accident, and a seriously handicapping disease.

Getting the Main Idea

Wilma has always worked on behalf of all her people—never merely in her own best interest.

Applying What You've Learned

Try to imagine what it would be like to lose all your family customs and traditions.

Rachel Carson

Remembering the Facts

1. *Silent Spring*
2. Pesticides
3. CBS
4. Springdale, Pennsylvania
5. *St. Nicholas*
6. Biology
7. Woods Hole, Massachusetts
8. Johns Hopkins University
9. *Albatross III*
10. *Under the Sea-Wind*

Understanding the Story

(Answers may vary)

1. Rachel loved the ocean; its plants and animals fascinated her.
2. She was against what pesticides do to the environment.

Getting the Main Idea

Rachel was not afraid to speak out when she felt an issue (no matter how big it might be to some businesspeople) placed the world's environment at risk.

Applying What You've Learned

Try to bring in economic factors and political interests as you discuss how you would argue on behalf of the future of the world.

DOROTHEA LANGE

Remembering the Facts

1. 17
2. She was a librarian.
3. Polio
4. Sophie
5. An orange
6. Arnold Genthe
7. Columbia University
8. San Francisco, California
9. One of Dorothea's most famous photographs of people waiting in line for free food
10. Maynard Dixon

Understanding the Story

(Answers may vary)

1. Because she spent so much time at her mother's work, watching the immigrants on the Lower East Side, and because an early bout of polio left her with a distinct limp
2. People fascinated Dorothea, and she photographed them to better understand their lives.

Getting the Main Idea

Dorothea did not take popular or pretty portraits. She took photos of the poor and underprivileged to persuade the government to better the living conditions for these people.

Applying What You've Learned

Identify the point you are trying to make, and then defend how you feel your photo or drawing best makes that point.

ROSALYN SUSSMAN YALOW

Remembering the Facts

1. It is an annual award granted to the person who has done the most to benefit the world community.
2. Alfred Nobel
3. Dynamite
4. Bronx, New York
5. Her mother's family was from Germany and her father's from the Ukraine.
6. Sewing
7. She turned the collars while her mother ironed them.
8. Hunter College
9. Secretarial
10. Radioimmunoassay

Understanding the Story

(Answers may vary)

1. Because she believed in what she was doing; she knew it could make a difference in extending people's lives.
2. They must always keep their minds open as they experiment with many different possibilities to find solutions to problems.

Getting the Main Idea

Because Rosalyn refused to give up when doors to further education and research jobs were rudely shut in her face

Applying What You've Learned

List the people you would acknowledge if you won a major award such as a Nobel Prize.

Ella Fitzgerald

Remembering the Facts

1. Newport News, Virginia
2. She worked as a cook and sometimes managed a laundry.
3. A dancer
4. Apollo
5. "The Object of My Affection"
6. Drums
7. "A Tisket, a Tasket"
8. Ella
9. Scat or bebop
10. Quintuple bypass surgery on her heart

Understanding the Story

(Answers may vary)

1. She always encouraged the talents of others.
2. It was an escape from other drab aspects of her life.

Getting the Main Idea

Ella Fitzgerald was one of America's legends, yet she always remained humble, considerate, and supportive of others.

Applying What You've Learned

List some of the steps you might have taken to avoid embarrassment in such a situation.

RUTH BADER GINSBERG

Remembering the Facts

1. In her high-school yearbook
2. 20
3. 12
4. Cornell University
5. Cancer
6. Fort Sill, Oklahoma
7. Because she was pregnant
8. Justice Felix Frankfurter
9. Rutgers
10. Bill Clinton

Understanding the Story

(Answers may vary)

1. Ruth became a strong advocate for equal rights and equal opportunities for women.
2. First, from her parents, then from her husband and children

Getting the Main Idea

Ruth never got discouraged by all the gender and religious bias she experienced.

Applying What You've Learned

Try to picture yourself as a social outcast and describe your feelings. Next, you should list ways in which you might be able to get above such prejudice.

KA'IULANI OF HAWAII

Remembering the Facts

1. October 16, 1875
2. He was her granduncle.
3. "The royal sacred one"
4. Princess Likelike
5. Scotland
6. Giant turtles and peacocks
7. 11
8. Robert Louis Stevenson
9. San Francisco, California
10. Grover Cleveland

Understanding the Story

(Answers may vary)

1. England; he said only there could she receive an education fit for a queen.
2. Because the Americans did not respect the native Hawaiians

Getting the Main Idea

As young and inexperienced as she was, the Princess did all that she could on behalf of her people. It took great courage for her to meet with the President of the United States.

Applying What You've Learned

List six of the most important characteristics for a good leader to have, and then explain why they are so critical.

BARBARA JORDAN

Remembering the Facts

1. She was a professor at the Lyndon B. Johnson School of Public Affairs.
2. Richard M. Nixon
3. House Judiciary Committee
4. Shred it
5. International (Debating) Platform Association
6. 1883
7. Houston, Texas
8. Lost
9. Boston University
10. Gender and racial

Understanding the Story

(Answers may vary)

1. She believed Texas was more than a state. She spoke of it as a frame of mind. She got a feeling from the soil and spirit of the state that she could accomplish whatever she wanted to do—that there were no limits.
2. She didn't notice because everyone else around her was just as poor.

Getting the Main Idea

Yes; African Americans need to feel the kind of pride that Jordan did—a pride born of enthusiasm and self-confidence.

Applying What You've Learned

List in one column some injustices you have observed in your school or community. Then, in the other column, list actions you might take or help to bring about to improve the situation for all involved.

DONNA KARAN

Remembering the Facts

1. Seventh Avenue
2. Model
3. Tailoring
4. "Popeye" or "Spaghetti Legs"
5. Parsons School of Design
6. Anne Klein
7. Her daughter
8. Sculptor
9. Bill Clinton
10. Designer of the Year

Understanding the Story

(Answers may vary)

1. Because her father was killed in an auto accident when she was just three years old, and her mother had to work so hard to support the family that Donna often felt abandoned by her
2. Because she was a working woman too, and she did not have hours to spend selecting clothes each day

Getting the Main Idea

Because she does not try to make women pretty on the outside; instead, she designs clothes that make women feel good on the inside, and feel independent and self-confident.

Applying What You've Learned

You could create outfits (from shoes on up) for all five days of the work week that would help make women feel comfortable and more confident about their abilities.

ELIZABETH COCHRANE SEAMAN
(NELLIE BLY)

Remembering the Facts

1. Elizabeth Cochrane Seaman
2. Stephen Foster
3. Pink
4. To become a teacher
5. *Pittsburgh Dispatch*
6. "What Girls Are Good For"
7. "The Lonely Orphan Girl"
8. "The Girl Puzzle"
9. Jules Verne
10. Blackwell's Island

Understanding the Story

(Answers may vary)

1. No, because she did improve conditions for working-class women and other less fortunate human beings around the world
2. Nellie exposed many injustices through her writing, and once they were brought to light, people often tried to do something to improve the situation.

Getting the Main Idea

She was not afraid to write about the truth, no matter how unflattering it might be, if exposing the truth could lead to reform.

Applying What You've Learned

List some ways in which you might draw attention to, or expose, certain intolerable living conditions to effect change.

NIKKI GIOVANNI

Remembering the Facts

1. Yolande Cornelia Giovanni, Jr.
2. *Black Feeling, Black Talk*
3. Knoxville, Tennessee
4. Louvenia
5. High-school English
6. Fisk University
7. Student Nonviolent Coordinating Committee
8. *Night Comes Softly*
9. *Truth Is on Its Way*
10. "Black Love Is Black Wealth"

Understanding the Story

(Answers may vary)

1. Because they had plenty of books and a piano in their house, and life was good
2. Her grandmother and her high-school English teacher

Getting the Main Idea

Because she believes the best way to deal with racial prejudice is to celebrate that life that people are biased against; her philosophy is to build up rather than tear down.

Applying What You've Learned

Think about what Nikki has given back to her people. Think about what kinds of things you could give back to your own community.

BONNIE BLAIR

Remembering the Facts

1. Five
2. Calgary, Canada
3. They did not like the fancy maneuvers in figure skating.
4. Three years old
5. Cornwall, New York
6. She raised the money on her own.
7. At a skating rink
8. 500-meter race
9. Calgary, Canada
10. *Sports Illustrated*

Understanding the Story

(Answers may vary)

1. She likes competing, skating as fast as she can.
2. She's highly encouraged by all the support.

Getting the Main Idea

She has the discipline to practice her skill and technique, and when she races she's out for her best race possible—not necessarily always to win but always to skate a *good* race.

Applying What You've Learned

Choose an Olympic event you would like to enter and describe what you think it would take to get there.

References

Helen Keller

Davidson, Margaret. *Helen Keller.* New York: Scholastic Inc., 1989.

Davidson, Margaret. *Helen Keller's Teacher.* New York: Scholastic Inc., 1992.

Lash, Joseph P. *Helen and Teacher: The Story of Helen Keller and Anne Sullivan Macy.* New York: Delacorte Press, 1980.

Peare, Catherine O. *The Helen Keller Story.* New York: HarperCollins, 1990.

St. George, Judith. *Dear Dr. Bell—Your Friend Helen.* New York: Putnam, 1992.

Eleanor Roosevelt

Cook, Blanche W. *Eleanor Roosevelt, Vol. I: 1884–1932.* New York: Viking, 1993.

Faber, Doris. *Eleanor Roosevelt: First Lady of the World.* New York: Viking, 1992.

Hershan, Stella K. *The Candles She Lit: The Legacy of Eleanor Roosevelt.* New York: Praeger, 1993.

Toor, Rachel. *Eleanor Roosevelt.* New York: Chelsea House, 1989.

Georgia O'Keeffe

Berry, Michael. *Georgia O'Keeffe*. New York: Chelsea House, 1988.

Buckley, Christopher. *Blossoms & Bones: On the Life and Work of Georgia O'Keeffe*. Nashville: Vanderbilt University Press, 1988.

Gherman, Beverly. *Georgia O'Keeffe: The "Wideness and Wonder" of Her World*. New York: Macmillan, 1986.

O'Keeffe, Georgia. *Georgia O'Keeffe: One Hundred Flowers*. New York: Knopf, 1989.

Julia Morgan

James, Cary. *Julia Morgan: Architect*. New York: Chelsea House, 1990.

Kett-O'Connor. *Julia Morgan*. Vero Beach, FL: Rourke, 1993.

Wadsworth, Ginger. *Julia Morgan: Architect of Dreams*. Minneapolis: Lerner, 1990.

Wilma P. Mankiller

Glassman, Bruce. *Wilma Mankiller: Chief of the Cherokee Nation*. Woodbridge, CT: Blackbirch, 1994.

Lazo, Caroline. *Wilma Mankiller*. New York: Dillon, 1994.

Mankiller, Wilma. *Wilma Mankiller: A Chief and Her People*. New York: St. Martins, 1994.

Yanuzzi, Della A. *Wilma Mankiller: Leader of the Cherokee Nation*. New York: Enslow, 1994.

Rachel Carson

Harlan, Judith. *Rachel Carson: Sounding the Alarm*. New York: Macmillan, 1989.

Henrickson, John. *Rachel Carson: The Environmental Movement*. Brookfield, CT: Millbrook Press, 1991.

Kudlinski, Kathleen. *Rachel Carson: Pioneer of Ecology*. New York: Viking, 1988.

Wadsworth, Ginger. *Rachel Carson: Voice for the Earth*. Minneapolis: Lerner, 1991.

Dorothea Lange

Cox, Christopher. *Dorothea Lange*. New York: Aperture, 1987.

Meltzer, Milton. *Dorothea Lange: Life Through the Camera*. New York: Viking, 1986.

Ohrn, Karin B. *Dorothea Lange and the Documentary Tradition*. Baton Rouge, LA: Louisiana State University Press, 1980.

Rosalyn Sussman Yalow

Dash, Joan. *The Triumph of Discovery: Women Scientists Who Won the Nobel Prize*. New York: Messner, 1991.

Ella Fitzgerald

Kliment, Bud. *Ella Fitzgerald*. New York: Chelsea House, 1989.

Wyman, Carolyn. *Ella Fitzgerald: Jazz Singer Supreme*. New York: Watts, 1993.

Ruth Bader Ginsberg

Roberts, Jack L. *Ruth Bader Ginsberg: Supreme Court Justice.* Brookfield, CT: Millbrook, 1994.

Ka'iulani of Hawaii

Stanley, Fay. *The Last Princess: The Story of Princess Ka'iulani of Hawaii.* New York: Four Winds, 1991.

Zambucka, Kristin. *Princess Ka'iulani: The Last Hope of Hawaii's Monarchy.* Kailua, HI: Mana, 1982.

Barbara Jordan

Haskins, James. *Barbara Jordan: Speaking Out.* New York: Dial, 1978.

Johnson, Linda. *Barbara Jordan: Congresswoman.* Woodbridge, CT: Blackbirch, 1994.

Jordan, Barbara. *Barbara Jordan: A Self-Portrait.* New York: Doubleday, 1979.

Roberts, Naurice. *Barbara Jordan: The Great Lady from Texas.* New York: Children's Press, 1984.

Donna Karan

Various magazine and newspaper articles.

Elizabeth Cochrane Seaman (Nellie Bly)

Ehrlich, Elizabeth. *Nellie Bly*. New York: Chelsea House, 1989.

Kendall, Martha E. *Nellie Bly: Reporter for the World*. Brookfield, CT: Millbrook, 1992.

Kroeger, Brooke. *Nellie Bly: Daredevil, Reporter, Feminist*. New York: Times Books, 1994.

Marks, Jason. *Around the World in Seventy-Two Days: The Race Between Pulitzer's Nellie Bly and Cosmopolitan's Elizabeth Bisland*. Gemittarius, 1993.

Nikki Giovanni

Fowler, Virginia C. *Nikki Giovanni*. New York: Macmillan, 1992.Fowler, Virginia C., ed. *Conversations with Nikki Giovanni*. Jackson, MS: University Press of Mississippi, 1992.

Giovanni, Nikki. *Gemini: An Extended Autobiographical Look at My First Twenty-Five Years of Being a Black Poet*. New York: Viking, 1976.

Giovanni, Nikki. *Knoxville, Tennessee*. New York: Scholastic Inc. 1994.

Bonnie Blair

Breitenbucher, Cathy. *Bonnie Blair: Golden Streak*. New York: Lerner, 1994.

Italia, Bob. *Bonnie Blair: Reaching for the Stars*. Minneapolis: Abdo & Daughters, 1994.

Rambeck, Richard. *Bonnie Blair*. New York: Childs World, 1995.

510 7 2/06

510 7 2/06